GANDHI IN CHAMPARAN

GANDHI
IN
CHAMPARAN

D. G. TENDULKAR

PUBLICATIONS DIVISION
MINISTRY OF INFORMATION AND BROADCASTING
GOVERNMENT OF INDIA

First Edition: 1957 (Saka 1879)
Reprinted: 1994 (Saka 1916)
Reprinted: 2005 (Saka 1927)
Restored Edition: 2017 (Saka 1938)

ISBN : 978 - 81 - 230 - 2392 - 2
GLI - ENG - REP - 180 - 2016-17

Price: ₹ 150/-

Published by the Addl. Director General, Publications Division,
Ministry of Information and Broadcasting,
Government of India, Soochna Bhawan, CGO Complex,
Lodhi Road, New Delhi- 110 003

Website: www.publicationsdivision.nic.in

THIS BOOK HAS NOW BEEN REPRODUCED, FROM THE 1957 EDITION OF THE PUBLICATIONS DIVISION, WITH THE HELP OF THE NATIONAL GANDHI MUSEUM, NEW DELHI. THIS RESTORED EDITION RETAINS THE ORIGINAL TEXT, VOLUME STRUCTURE, LINE STRUCTURE, ETC.

Sales Centres: Soochna Bhawan, CGO Complex, Lodhi Road, **New Delhi**-110 003 ● Hall No.196, Old Secretariat, **Delhi**-110054 ● 701, C-Wing, 7th Floor, Kendriya Sadan, CBD, Belapur, **Navi Mumbai**-400614 ● 8, Esplanade East, **Kolkata**-700069 ● A' Wing, F-Block, Ground Floor, Rajaji Bhawan, Besant Nagar, **Chennai**-600090 ● Press Road, Near Govt. Press, **Thiruvananthapuram**-695001 ● Room No. 204, 2nd Floor, C.G.O. Towers, Kavadiguda, **Hyderabad**-500080. ● Ist Floor, 'F' Wing, Kendriya Sadan, Koramangala, **Bangalore**-560034 ● Bihar State Co-operative Bank Building, Ashoka Rajpath, **Patna**-800004 ● Hall No.1, 2nd Floor, Kendriya Bhawan, Sector-H, Aliganj, **Lucknow**-226024 ● Ambica Complex, 1st Floor, Above UCO Bank, Paldi, **Ahmedabad**-380007 ● House No.07, Cheni Kuthi, New Colony, K.K.B. Road, **Guwahati**-781003

Processed at : National Gandhi Museum, New Delhi
Printed at : J.K. Offset Graphics Pvt. Ltd., New Delhi

FOREWORD

THIS small book with a simple title contains the forty-year old story of Gandhiji's first satyagraha on Indian soil. Accounts of that satyagraha have appeared in various forms, one of them written by no less a personage than Dr. Rajendra, Prasad, who joined Gandhiji as a co-worker even as early that campaign. That story is narrated here over again, but it has been enriched by the author with fresh material from Government and other records which were not available earlier. Shri D. G. Tendulkar visited the area and gathered some information from local sources also. The general reader is sure to find this new book on an old subject inviting. The theme is such that it can lose neither its lesson nor its interest.

The scene is laid in the district of Champaran in North Bihar. The occasion was Gandhiji's first attempt in India to remove, by truthful and Non-violent means, the grievances and sufferings of the simple peasants at the hands of the indigo planters, who were often supported by the rulers of the day. As he came more and more in contact with Bihar, Gandhiji began to love "the humility, simplicity, goodness and extraordinary faith so characterstic of the Biharis".

Gandhiji discovered, as early as 1908, what he called the sovereign remedy of satyagraha, in the course of his successful leadership of the Indians in South Africa in their hard and prolonged struggle against a number of inquties based on racial discrimination at the hands of the white residents as well as the rulers. He evoked what he called soul-force in contrast to physical force. He did so out of conviction that it was the best way and the way of cultured humanity.

At Germiston in South Africa, while challenging Mr. Hosken, who said that passive resistance was a weapon of the weak, Gandhiji defined his passive resistance as "soul-force" and added that it was the weapon of the stongest. He told his audience that brute force had no place in the programme of the Indians, even if there was a possibility of using it. Gandhiji pointed out that even if they had arms he would have advised Indians to use soul-force only. In planning satyagraha in South Africa, he asserted that even the slightest thought about the use of physical force did not touch him at any time and at any stage. He pitted moral force against physical force because he believed that it was a superior force. He refrained from the use of physical force, direct or indirect. He trained thousands to do so. He would not even think in terms of any injury to his opponents; on the other hand, he would go to the ends of the earth to do good to them. Gandhiji always aimed his blows at the evil in the evil-doer. The evil-doer continued to be the object of his love and friendship.

This was, then, the meaning of Gandhiji's ahimsa in thought, word and deed. With him, ahimsa and satyagraha were not ways and weapons of the weak but of the strongest in spirit. In his speech on September 11, 1906, in South Africa he said : "But I can boldly declare, and with certainty, that so long as there are even a handful of men true to their pledge, there can be only one end to the struggle, and that is victory." His faith in this new way of combating human wrongs, evils, iniquities and injustice, whether social, economic or political, individual or national, grew as he preached and practised it in South Africa.

He did not think that his fight on these lines in South Africa was an isolated one or of no consequence. He was as much aware of its newness as of its universal applicability. To the Rev. Mr. Doke, his first biographer in South Africa, he wrote in 1908, when asked for a message: "I regard it as an absolutely sure remedy, not only for our ills in the Transvaal but for all the political and other troubles from which our people suffer in India." His newly-discovered letter to Tolstoy on November 10, 1909, has this remarkable passage : "In my opinion, this struggle of the Indians in the Transvaal is the greatest of modern times, inasmuch as it has been idealised both as to the goal as also the methods adopted to reach the goal. I am not aware of a struggle in which the participators are not to derive any personal advantage at the end of it. . . If it succeeds, it will be not only a triumph of religion, love and truth over irreligion, hatred and falsehood, but it is highly likely to serve as an example to the millions in India and to people in other parts of the world who may be down-trodden, and will certainly go a great way towards breaking up the party of violence, at least in India."

It was with this firm and mature faith that he came to India. He took up the case of the Viramgam customs cordon, which was a source of great harassment, and succeeded in getting it removed by merely publishing the absurdity of the wrong and writing to the Government about it. The next gross injustice that he took up for remedying was the curse of Indian indentured labour. He carried on a correspondence with the then Governor-General and told him that satyagraha might follow if such a flagrant injustice was not brought to a stop. He succeeded in this case also. Then came the call from Champaran through Rajkumar Shukla, a son of the soil, whose heart spoke to Gandhiji in a language which was full of anguish and sincerity. Gandhiji responded, and the story in this book was the result.

Gandhiji's way of dealing with all evil and injustice is obviously a new one. It is rooted in the faith that all life is one, that love is the law of life and that love alone which builds life and is a positive force can effectively conquer injustice, hatred and violence, which are negative forces destroying life.

In the words of Mr. Homer Jack, an American author, satyagraha is truly "an epochal social invention". It is war without violence against all that represents the forces of evil and violence. It is meant for all and not merely for saints. It is a weapon of the strong and not of the weak.

It is in establishing this truth of truths that Gandhiji is at once original and one who has gone beyond all prophets before him. Gandhiji does not recognise any exception to the rule that satyagraha is a sovereign remedy against all evils and is applicable under every circumstance. He makes no distinction between secular and religious, material and spiritual, practical and ideal spheres of activity so far as the application of satyagraha is concerned. If, for the time being, a Satyagrahi does not see his way, it is the temporary incapacity of the person and not the inapplicability of the doctrine. "Let him knock and the door shall be opened." This infinite faith of Gandhiji was rooted in his inner spiritual experience of the immanent presence of Truth or God.

Satyagraha knows no defeat, Gandhiji often emphasised. Satyagraha may be said to succeed best when the evil-doer or the perpetrator of injustice realizes his folly, repents and makes amends in all sincerity. This would be called a case of genuine and complete conversion. But there are other ways also in which satyagraha may succeed. The evil-doer may retrace his steps out of shame on account of the awakening of his own conscience and the pressure of public opinion. It may also be that he will be induced to desist from continuing the wrong out of discretion and practical wisdom. There is also another way in which satyagraha may succeed indirectly, when the evil-doer may be forced by the powers that be to desist from wrong-doing. It may also happen that a satyagrahi loses his life in the attempt to establish peace and the law of love. Even this would, in the eyes of Gandhiji, be a triumph of satyagraha since the satyagrahi's martyrdom would be the seed for future resistance, which one day was bound to triumph. He declared that life persists in spite of death and light persists in spite of darkness, and that truth must triumph over falsehood, and good over evil.

It was very fortunate that the Bihar Government was able to get Shri D. G. Tendulkar, the well-known author of *'Mahatma'* in eight volumes, to write this story. It is equally fortunate that the Central Ministry of Information and Broadcasting has taken upon itself the publication of this work in the present attractive form. It is my good fortune to be in a position to congratulate the Bihar Government through its Chief Minister, Dr. S. K. Sinha, for deciding to bring out this book and inviting Shri Tendulkar to write it. I am glad to see that Shri Tendulkar has been able to spare the time for this important assignment.

I commend this book to all who are interested in social dynamics and in a peaceful solution of human conflicts, leading to the harmony and happiness of all.

R. R. Diwakar

Patna
June 7, 1957

INTRODUCTION

GANDHI was described as an "unwelcome visitor" when he reached South Africa in 1893, at the age of twenty-four. For twenty years he worked there among the indentured labourers, lightened their sorrows, organized them and kindled the flame of consciousness of human rights throughout the dark continent by leading the first epic march of 2,037 men, 127 women and 57 children in November 1913, in protest against the ill-treatment of Indians in South Africa. Tolstoy wrote : "Your activity in Transvaal is the most essential work, the most important of all the works now being done in the world, wherein the nations of all the world will unavoidably take part." The satyagraha struggle closed triumphantly in 1914 and Gandhi returned to India in January 1915. At the request of Gokhale, he did not participate in any activity for a year but studied closely the conditions in India and took his first plunge in 1917 in champaran. Although he was not then a big figure in the political arena, he was known as a hero of South Africa throughout India. To remove the indigo cultivators' grievances was his objective. The authorities told him that he was an outsider and he had no business in Champaran, but he defied them. Within a year he washed away the century-old stain of indigo and forged a weapon with which he broke the shackles of slavery and made India free in thirty years.

The Champaran struggle, therefore forms an important chapter in India's non-violent war of independence. If my book *Mahatma* is a panorama of the Gandhian era in eight large volumes, the present slender volume is a close-up of the earliest phase of that struggle.

Satyagraha in Champaran by Rajendra Prasad give a detailed and authentic account of this struggle. With his kind encouragement I am supplementing his narration with the unpublished material marked as "confidential" by the British Government in India. Most of the confidential documents relating to India's freedom movement were burnt by the British before they transferred power to Indian hands. The material now in possession of the Bihar Government which I have used was left untouched through the carelessness of some official who had orders to bum it. It is valuable material which gives insight into the British administration and helps to reconstruct the momentous history of the Champaran campaign.

Besides the confidential documents and Rajendra Babu's book I have used the files of *Pioneer* and the *Statesman* and other journals. Gandhiji's autobiography has helped me to reconstruct some scenes in the struggle which even today stand out as touching and intimate and give an insight into his methods.

In giving an account of the long-standing grievances of the indigo workers I have made use of the authentic material in *History of Indigo Disturbance in Bengal* by L. C. Mitra, *Bengal under the Lieutenant-Governors* by C. E Buckland and *The Report of the Committee on the Agrarian Conditions in Champaran*.

The Government of Bihar and the Governor, Shri R. R. Diwakar, have given me an opportunity and ample facilities to write this book and I thank them for it.

I must mention the libraries which supplied me with rare literature, such as *Nil Durpan*, available only at the National Library, Calcutta. In perusing the files of the *Statesman* and *Pioneer* I was helped by Anu Bandyopadhyaya. The Branch of the Royal Asiatic Society's Library in Bombay was helpful in allowing me to use the files of journals which are not available even with the offices of the journals concerned. I also made use of the Sinha Library in Patna. My thanks are due to my friend Vithalbhai K. Jhaveri for throwing open to me his rich collection of books concerning Gandhiji.

Lastly, I am grateful to the colleagues of Gandhiji in Champaran who helped me to visit the scenes of the struggle and collect the necessary material: Ramnavmi Prasad, Ramdayal Sahu and Harivans Sahay.

I thank K. K. Nambiar for typing the manuscript under heavy odds. For reading the manuscript I am grateful to my friends Shamlal and M. Chalapathi Rau.

D. G. TENDULKAR

Bombay, 1955

CONTENTS

LIST OF ILLUSTRATIONS

Cover design by Vithalbhai K. Jhaveri

INDIGO STAIN

THE TALE of woes of Indian ryots, forced to plant indigo by the British planters, forms one of the blackest chapters in the annals of colonial exploitation. "Not a chest of indigo reached England without being stained with human blood," said Mr. E. De-Latour of the Bengal Civil Service, who was Magistrate of Faridpur in 1848. Giving evidence before an inquiry committee, he revealed: "I have seen several ryots sent unto me as a magistrate, who have been speared through the body. I have had ryots before me who have been shot down by Mr. Forde, a planter. I have put on record how others have been first speared and then kidnapped; and such a system of carrying on indigo, I consider a system of bloodshed."

Indigo was one of the oldest, and, until the introduction of tea-planting, ranked as the most important of the Indian staples grown by European capital. In 1877-78 the total export of indigo from India was 120,605 cwt., valued at £ 3,494,334; in 1878-79, 105,051 cwt., valued at £ 2,960,463; in 1882-83 the export of indigo was 141,041 cwt., of the value of £ 3,912,997.

It is difficult to say when exactly indigo was first cultivated in India, but it appears from records that it had been well known for long as an indigenous product of India. Brought thence to Europe, as a favourite dye and prized article of commerce, according to ancient authors, it derived its name of "Indicum" from the country in which it grew.

In the year 1600, indigo was the main staple by which the East India Company made its profits and for many years it fostered the trade. At one period it was found to grow better in the West Indies and after carrying on the trade for a century, the East India Company gave up indigo as an article of investment in favour of the West India colonies. But in the West Indies it was found to be less profitable than other crops, and was given up and again taken up by the East India Company who, having lost £ 80,000 in 1779 by contract, made it over to its servants and to private traders. The East India Company, with a view to fostering intensive cultivation of indigo in India, advanced enormous sums to the white planters.

The planters resorted to inhuman and illegal methods in order to get indigo cultivated at the lowest cost. Sir Ashley Eden in his evidence before the Indigo Commission of 1860 gave a list of their heinous acts and added that even justice was traversed when the planters were put on trial. When asked by the commission as to why this happened, Sir Ashley Eden said : "There certainly was a failure of justice which, in my opinion, may, to a great extent, be attributed to the strong bias which the Governor and many of the officers of the Government have always displayed in favour of those engaged in this particular cultivation; this may also partly have arisen from the difficulty, which exists under the present law, of obtaining a conviction against Europeans. I consider that it has frequently been the case that the Government officials have sacrificed justice to favour the planters. I will go further and say that, as a young assistant, I confess I have favoured my own countrymen in several instances."

The suspicion of the ryots as to the collusion between the Government and planters was roused, when in 1857, the Government of Sir Frederick Halliday appointed some of the leading planters in the districts of Krishnagore and Murshidabad to be assistant magistrates. The Rev. J. W. Lincke of Krishnagore, who mixed freely with the ryots there, told the inquiry commission that the impression was very unfavourable among the ryots. "Now they have made the wolf the shepherd of the sheep," was a popular saying among them at this time. The Rev. James Long said he even heard songs condemnatory of planters as magistrates, set to music and sung by a band of singers in the Krishnagore district.

There was even an impression that the Lieutenant-Governor, Sir Frederick Halliday, had a share in some of the indigo concerns. Many officials and planters mixed freely and obliged one another. But there were solitary exceptions also, such as in the case of the Lieutenant-Governor of Bengal, Sir John Peter Grant, and his Secretary, Mr. W. S. Seton-Karr. A minute by Sir John on the report of the Indigo Commission states:

"The records of Government show that the system of indigo manufacture in the Province of Bengal has been unsound from a very early time... Substantially, the system at the beginning of the present year was as false as ever it had been. In the year 1810, the licences granted to four planters to reside in the interior of the country were withdrawn, on account of the severe ill-usage of the natives proved against them;

and the Governor-General-in-Council found it necessary to issue a circular in that year, of date the 13th of July, from which the following is an extract :

" 'The attention of Government has recently been attracted in a particular manner to abuses and oppressions committed by Europeans who are established as indigo planters in different parts of the country. Numerous as those abuses and oppressions have latterly been, the Right Hon'ble the Governor-General-in-Council is still willing to hope that this imputation does not attach to the character of the indigo planters generally, considered as a body or class of people. The facts, however, which have recently been established against some individuals of that class before the magistrates and the Supreme Court of Judicature are of so flagrant a nature that the Governor-General-in-Council considers it an act of indispensable public duty to adopt such measures as appear to him, under existing circumstances, best calculated to prevent the repetition of offences equally injurious to the English character and to the peace and happiness of our native subjects.'

"The offences to which the following remarks refer, and which have been established beyond all doubt or dispute by individual indigo planters, may be reduced to the following heads :

"First, acts of violence, which, although they amount not in the legal sense of the word to murder, have occasioned the death of natives.

"Secondly, the illegal detention of natives in confinement, especially in stocks, with a view to the recovery of balances alleged to be due from them or for other causes.

"Thirdly, assembling, in a tumultuary manner, the people attached to their respective factories, and others, and engaging in violent affrays with other indigo planters.

"Fourthly, illicit infliction of punishment, by means of a rattan or otherwise, on the cultivators or other natives.

"The magistrates were directed by the same circular to cause stocks kept by planters to be destroyed; to report to Government cases of illegal corporal punishment not sufficient to warrant a commitment to the Supreme Court; and to impress on all Europeans who wished to continue to reside in the country the necessity of abstaining from ill-treatment of the people.

"In a subsequent circular, of 22nd July 1810, magistrates were directed to report all proved instances of planters who were convicted of "obliging the ryots who reside in the vicinity of their respective factories to receive advances, and of adopting other illicit and improper means to compel them to cultivate indigo'; the Governor-General-in-Council observing that this was a 'habit' of the planters."

The Lieutenant-Governor further said in his minute:

"When the ryot has a zamindar, who is not an indigo manufacturer, he has some protector in indigo matters. When the same man is indigo manufacturer and zamindar, or zamindar's representative, the ryot has no such protection.

"It is indeed in itself an all-sufficient exposition of the character of the Bengal indigo system to state, what is denied by none, that, whilst within a few years the prices of all agricultural products have doubled or nearly doubled, the price paid or nominally paid for indigo plant has not been raised by a single anna; and that until the ryots had, as it were, declared open war, it is not shown that a single planter, for several years past, had ever entertained thought of any increase of price. . .

"The Indigo Commission report that the crisis which occurred in 1860 might have occurred in any other year. The combined effect of all the foregoing considerations upon my mind is that no human power exerted in defiance of the law in support of the system could have upheld it much longer; and that, if Government had disregarded justice and policy so far as to make an attempt, it would have been speedily punished by a great agrarian rising, the destructive effect of which upon European and all other capital no man can calculate...

"The commissioners pronounce conclusively that the cultivation is unprofitable to the ryot. This is indeed the one point upon which the whole indigo question runs; and it is not disputed. Rejecting all extreme cases, and giving indigo the benefit of all doubts, I cannot put the absolute loss to the ryot at a low average, reckoning the net loss in the cultivation of indigo at the highest price now allowed, and the loss of the net profit the ryot would make by any other ordinary crop at the market price, at less than Rs. 7 a bigha, equivalent at the least to seven times the rent of the land. Now, if one remembers that these ryots are not Carolina slaves, but the free yeomanry of this country, and indeed, strictly speaking, the virtual owners of the greater part of the land in the old cultivated parts of Bengal, so heavy a loss as this will fully account to us for the strength of the opposition to indigo cultivation which we have just experienced...This is the great point of political bearing in the whole question, and it cannot be too attentively considered by all who have any responsibility for the tranquillity of the country, and the strength of the British Government within it. If any one thinks that such a demonstration of strong feeling by hundreds of thousands of people, as we have just witnessed in Bengal, has no meaning of greater importance than an ordinary commercial question concerning a particular blue dye, such a person, in my opinion, is fatally mistaken in the signs of the time."

The disputes connected with indigo cultivation in Bengal had long been a subject of anxiety to Government. In 1860 the excitement against the cultivation of indigo had become so strong as to lead to acts of violence in some of the indigo districts, and things looked very critical. "I assure you," wrote Lord Canning, the Viceroy, "that for about a week it caused me more anxiety than I had since the days of Delhi," and, "from that day I felt that a shot fired in anger or fear by one foolish planter might put up every factory in flames."

Sir J. P. Grant, the Lieutenant-Governor of Bengal, who was on tour along the Kumar and the Kaliganga rivers has given a vivid description of awakening among the indigo workers in 1860 :

"Numerous crowds of ryots appeared at various places on the banks of the Kumar and the Kaliganga, whose whole prayer was for an order of Government that they should not cultivate indigo. On my return a few days afterwards along the same two rivers, from dawn to dusk, as I steamed along these two rivers for some sixty or seventy miles, both banks were literally lined with crowds of villagers, claiming justice in this matter. Even the women of the villages on the banks were collected in groups by themselves; the males who stood at and between the river-side villages in little crowds must have collected from all the villages at a great distance on either side. I do not know that it ever fell to the lot of any Indian officer to steam for fourteen hours through a continued double street of suppliants for justice; all were most respectful and orderly, and also were plainly in earnest. It would be folly to suppose that such a display on the part of tens of thousands of people, men, women, and children, has no deep meaning. The organization and capacity for combined and simultaneous action in the cause, which this remarkable demonstration over so large an extent of country proved, are subjects worthy of much consideration."

The ryots had told the Indigo Commission : "But if my throat is cut, I won't sow indigo"; "I would rather go to a country where the indigo plant is never seen or sown"; "I would sow indigo for nobody, not even for my father and mother"; "No, I would be rather killed with bullets."

The feelings of the ryots were also voiced in their songs and sayings. A Bengali book of songs entitled *The Oppression of the Indigo Planters* was widely circulated. Those songs were sung far and wide among the indigo ryots and set to music.

The Rev. S. J. Hill of the London Missionary Society repeated before the Indigo Inquiry Commission the following verse of a ballad, sung widely in Bengali:

Zaminer Shatru Nil
Kormer Shatru Dhil
Temoni Jater Shatru Padre Hill.

(The enemy of the soil is indigo; The enemy of labour is idleness; So the enemy of caste is Padre Hill.)

Sufferings of the ryots were graphically depicted in *Nil Durpan,* a Bengali drama written by Dinabandhu Mitra in 1860. In Nadia the author's birthplace, it was whispered that a beautiful peasant girl was carried off one day, while going to fetch water, by a planter's servant to oblige the manager of an indigo factory. It was alleged that the manager had kept her in his room till midnight and then sent her back in a palki with closed doors. This story was told by a missionary before the Indigo Commission and verified by the magistrate. The scene of abduction and many other moving scenes of oppression in *Nil Durpan* were based on facts found in the indigo areas.

The drama was meant to mirror the stern realities of the indigo worker's life and it was called "the mirror of indigo", *Nil Durpan.* The play stated the point of view of the ryot forced to grow indigo at a price that did not pay him. In the course of the play, the wife of a peasant says to another village woman: "Moreover, the wife of the planter, in order to make her husband's case strong, has sent a letter to the magistrate since it is said that the magistrate hears her words most attentively."

"I saw the lady," replies the other, "she has no shame at all. When the magistrate goes riding about the villages, the lady also rides on horseback with him. Riding a horse !"

Dinabandhu Mitra did not give his name in the book which was described as "written by a certain traveller for the good of ryots suffering from the bite of the cobra-de-capello in the form of the indigo planter."

The author was then in the service of the Government as superintendent under the Post Master General, Bengal. He had to go from village to village inspecting post offices. He used to meet people of all classes. He had travelled much in those districts where indigo was manufactured, and was acquainted in all its details with the oppression of the ryots by the planters of that time. During his inspection tours, he composed the celebrated play. One night, while writing the drama on a sinking boat, he clung to the manuscript and it was saved.

Referring to the author, Bankim Chandra Chatterjee, the great Bengali novelist, says : "I have known none other touch the heart of the sorrows of the poor and the afflicted as he did. By virtue of his natural sympathy, the misery of the oppressed ryot appealed to his heart like misery felt by himself, and the poet was constrained to pour out the fountain of his heart through his pen. Though the chief aim of *Nil Durpan* was the correction of a social wrong, still it was most excellent as a piece of poetic art."

Nil Durpan was read with great eagerness all over Bengal. The Rev. James Long took upon himself the task of having the drama translated in English to acquaint the Government and the British community with the sentiments of the Indian people. The translation was made by the gifted poet Michael Madhusudan Dutt in one night. The translator's name was not mentioned in the book; the Rev. James Long published the book and wrote an introduction under his own name.

In the introduction to the translation the Rev. James Long described the play as "the annals of the poor" and added: "It pleads the cause of those who are feeble; it describes a respectable ryot, a peasant proprietor, happy with his family in the enjoyment of his land till the indigo system compels him to take advances, to neglect his own land, cultivate crops which beggared him, reducing him to the condition of a serf and a vagabond; the effects of this on his home, children and relatives are pointed out in a language, plain but true; it shows how arbitrary power debases the lord as well as the peasant; reference is also made to the partiality of various magistrates in favour of planters and to the act of the last year penally enforcing indigo contracts."

The translation was circulated with the sanction of the Secretary to the Government of Bengal, Mr. W. S. Seton-Karr. Out of 500 copies printed, only about 200 were circulated in England and 14 in India. The Landholders' and Commercial Association through their secretary, Mr. W. F. Fergusson, addressed Government asking whether the publication had been circulated with the sanction and authority of the Government of Bengal, and for the names and parties who had circulated "a foul and malicious libel on indigo planters tending to excite sedition and breaches of the peace" with a view to their prosecution. In the correspondence which ensued Government pointed out that indigo planters were not the only class, Indian or European, criticized in the play; as faults had been imputed as unsparingly to European magistrates, Indian officials, and Indian factory supervisors, as to indigo planters. "It has no interest but as an indication of strong popular feeling," said Government. "As such, however, it has significance. The knowledge of respectable official or other European gentlemen of the existence of such indication of popular feeling as this be anything but a security against actual sedition and breaches of the peace." In expressing regret for the official transmission of the translation in question, the Government said : "The position of indigo planters in some Bengal districts at present is one with which the Government sincerely sympathizes. And nothing is more earnestly desired than the speedy introduction of a sound system for the future, such as shall carry native feeling along with it."

The planters were furious and the Landholders' and Commercial Association decided to prosecute the people connected with the publication of *Nil Durpan.* Mr. Manuel, the printer of the translation, was prosecuted in the Supreme Court for libel, and fined. As the name of the translator was not mentioned in the book, the Reverend Mr. Long, who had superintended the translation of the play, was fined and imprisoned for a month by the same court. The Rev. James Long said : "If I suffer in this cause, it will only be in common with far worthier men who have suffered the loss of all things in the cause of truth, righteousness and humanity."

Mr. Seton-Karr submitted an apology to the Government of India.

The Secretary of State, who had stated his entire disapproval of the circulation of the translation under the official seal and frank of the Bengal Government, agreed that Mr. Seton-Karr should not be allowed to resume his secretaryship, but expressed no doubt that "so able and distinguished a public servant as Mr. Seton-Karr will, on his ceasing to sit in the Legislative Council, be placed in some suitable situation where the public may have the benefit of his service."

For championing the cause of the ryots, the indigo planters launched a campaign against Sir John Peter Grant, the Lieutenant-Governor of Bengal. They attacked him with virulence through the Anglo-Indian press, describing him as "a terrible man—a compound of Ghengis and Kublai Khan, Tamerlane, Nadir and all". They appealed to the Governor-General and Secretary of State to remove Sir John Grant from his high office. Sir John broke down in implementing his bold indigo measures, owing to stubborn opposition from the higher authorities. He retired in 1862 and soon after was sued by a planter for libel. The planter was awarded nominal damages of one rupee without costs.

The echoes of *Nil Durpan* spread far and wide. The excitement was not confined to Bengal only. A protest was lodged in India and England through the press and public meetings against the Rev. Long's incarceration. The drama was staged in some Indian cities and was translated in many languages of Europe. When it was staged in Calcutta, Vidyasagar, a highly respected leader of Bengal, got so worked up that he threw his shoe during a scene of oppression on the stage. In fact, *Nil Durpan* like *Uncle Tom's Cabin* won the sympathy of the people for the cause of the downtrodden.

ROCKS AHEAD

THE INDIGO trouble, which had subsided in Nadia and Jessore districts, came up again in Bihar which until 1911 formed a part of the Bengal Province.

Some disputes arose during the year 1866-67 between the ryots and the manager of the Pandoul indigo factory in the Darbhanga Estate in Tirhut. Though the question only came to a head in one concern, the report of the local officers, the general anxiety among planters, the number of petitions submitted, and the agitation of the Indian press indicated that the crisis was a serious one. The principal points at issue were as follows: The factory maintained that in addition to the *nijabad* indigo lands, or lands undoubtedly in possession of the factory and cultivated by factory ploughs, there were in every village other lands equally in the possession of the factory which were planted with indigo for the factory by the ryots, and in respect of which the ryots were not cultivators of indigo in their own lands for the factory under contract, but merely hired labourers cultivating *zerait* lands on behalf of the factory and receiving wages in return. The ryots, on the other hand, asserted that the lands thus described were not factory *zerait,* but formed part of their own proper holdings ; that the factory people prevented them from cultivating these with cereals and other crops which paid them better than indigo by falsely claiming these lands as *zerait* and accusing the ryots of criminal trespass when they attempted to cultivate them in the manner they liked best ; that they were also very much oppressed by their ploughs and bullocks being taken away from them during the manufacturing season for the purposes of the factory, and that, while the factory leased villages from the Darbhanga Estate on the same rent as before, the rates levied from the cultivators had been considerably enhanced by the introduction of a system of sub-letting the villages to the factory servants who were rapacious in their demands. The result of these differences was that the ryots of a number of villages, who had up to the occurrence of the disputes been engaged in preparing the lands for indigo, suddenly united together in refusing either to finish the preparation of the lands or to allow the factory to do so. This led to collisions with the planters' servants. Government stepped in, the necessity of increasing the rates paid for indigo was recognized by several of the Tirhut planters, and the Pandoul ryots came to terms with the factory.

A year later there was a strong demonstration in the district of Champaran, accompanied by violence. The causes of dissatisfaction on the part of the ryots were the unusual trouble and the hard labour involved in the cultivation of indigo; the harassment caused to the ryots by the factory servants who, besides committing other acts of oppression, were in the habit of taking a very large percentage of the payments made to the ryots as their own perquisites under the general name of *dasturi*; the fact that the rates which were then being paid for indigo cultivation did not give adequate remuneration for the labour expended on the task ; the widespread knowledge existing among cultivators that enormous profits were derived from indigo, and the natural desire on their part to obtain a larger share of this profit.

The opposition of the ryots showed itself by the exhibition of a general determination not to sow indigo, and in some cases by the forcible appropriation of the lands already prepared for the cultivation of indigo to other crops. The first instance of such exhibition occurred in a village called Jaukatia, the ryots of which, in defiance of the contract into which they had entered with the Lalsaraiya factory, sowed their lands with cold-weather crops; and this example was rapidly followed by other villagers.

The disputes between the ryots and the planters threatened to become serious. The ryots were determined not to sow indigo unless they received better treatment at the hands of the planters. The local officers almost unanimously reported that the cultivation of indigo had become absolutely unpopular, and that there was not a ryot who would not abandon its cultivation if he could. This unpopularity was ascribed as much to the insufficiency of the remuneration which the ryots received, as to the exactions, oppression, and annoyance to which they were exposed at the hands of the factory servants. The Government was satisfied that the time had passed when the planters could hope to carry on an indigo concern profitably by forcing on the ryots a cultivation and labour which was unprofitable to them; and it was clear that in the altered circumstances of the time the planters must be prepared either to close their factories or to give to the ryots a remuneration which should make it worth their while to grow indigo.

This necessity was recognized by the general body of the Tirhut and Champaran planters, and they yielded to the pressure, raising the rate of remuneration from Rs. 7-8-0 to Rs. 12 per bigha.

In the face of united opposition the planters yielded for a while, but the oppression continued. The planters belonged to the race of the ruling class and they were connected with the local officers by ties of marriage or at least of friendship and sympathy. The planter treated the ryots like slaves. He let out land to peasants on condition that they agreed not only to pay rent but to grow indigo on a quarter of their land. He gave them advances and he saw to it that the ryots were never able to repay in full. Thus they were his debtors, as well as his tenants.

The pioneer of the indigo industry in Bihar was Francois Grand, Collector of Tirhut in the years 1782-85, who has left it on record that he introduced the manufacture of indigo after the European manner, encouraged the establishment of indigo works and plantations and erected three at his own expense. Thirty years elapsed before the cultivation of indigo by European methods was introduced into Champaran. The first factory in the district was founded in 1813 at Bara by Colonel Hickey. Shortly afterwards, the Rajpur and Turkaulia concerns were started and the cultivation was steadily extended. In 1830 the collector urged the construction of roads for the development of commerce and reported that the Government would be able to avail themselves of the assistance of indigo planters. During the first half of the century, however, indigo had to yield precedence to sugar, the manufacture of which was the premier industry of Champaran, steam sugar factories being scattered over a large area. About 1850, the high prices obtained for indigo dealt a severe blow at this industry, the cultivation of sugar was replaced by indigo, and sugar factories were converted into indigo concerns.

During the flourishing days of the indigo industry two systems of cultivation were followed: *zerait* and *asamiwar*. The term *zerait* has often been incorrectly applied to any land in the direct occupation of a factory, and not only the land held by a proprietor or superior tenure-holder. *Zerait* indigo land was cultivated by the factory at its own expense and with hired labour. *Asamiwar* means cultivation through tenants of factory. Roughly, one-third of the cultivation was carried on under the *zerait* system and two-thirds under the *asamiwar* system.

The *zerait* system of cultivation returned the best profits. The factory owners under this system used to cultivate the land in their possession with the help of their own ploughs and bullocks. This land used to be either the proprietor's private land or land in which the factory owner had acquired rights of occupancy. The entire burden of cultivation used to be on the factory. The only connection that the tenants had with this cultivation was that they were liable to render service on the land or to have their bullocks and their ploughs impressed for indigo cultivation under the orders of the factory. No factory was fully self-contained in the matter of cultivating its land.

When the system of *asamiwar* cultivation was followed, the indigo was grown by factory tenants, under the direction of the factory's servants, at fixed rates per bigha. Generally documents called *sattas* were executed, the ryot receiving an advance and binding himself to grow indigo on a certain specified portion of his holding, and to pay damages, *harja,* if he should fail to carry out his contract. All the expenses of cultivation were paid by the ryot, but the seed was supplied by the factory, which also cut and carted away the indigo, the ryot being paid for the services at fixed rates. When the *sattas* were executed, the cultivators had to agree for a term of years, sometimes twenty to thirty years, to grow indigo on three *kathas* per bigha of their holdings. This was called the *tinkathia* system, which led to constant friction between the ryots and the planters.

The third system, which was uncommon in Champaran, was *khuski* or cultivation by means of agreements with outside ryots. In this case the factory supplied the seed and paid for the crop when delivered, at privileged rates. This system was rarely adopted by the Champaran factories because they had extensive tenure-holding rights and they could make better terms with their own ryots.

The *kurtauli* system of cultivation also came into existence in 1880. Under it the ryot mortgaged his entire holding and the very site of his house for a period probably extending beyond his own life-time, redemption being contingent on the repayment of the loan. The ryot sold himself body and soul into hopeless servitude. This system was not widely prevalent in Champaran.

In the early days indigo factories were started only in places where the soil was fit for indigo and sugarcane cultivation. In about 1875, when they had established their influence fully, the Europeans also began to settle in the north-western part of the Champaran district. The soil being unfit for indigo cultivation, they had to find suitable lands somewhere else. For building factories they took small lands on perpetual lease from the Bettiah Raj, extending over 2,000 square miles, which had become heavily involved in debt owing to the extravagance of the ruler. Mr. T. Gibbon, Manager of the Raj, raised a sterling loan of about Rs. 95 lakhs in England on the condition of substantial European security. To satisfy this condition and cover the interest on the loan, it was agreed that the Bettiah Raj should settle a portion of its estate with European factory owners in perpetuity, and they would be paid the reserved rent towards the liquidation of the debt. Accordingly, lands fetching five lakhs and a half per year were settled in perpetual or *mokarri* lease with fourteen factories. This permanent interest in the land strengthened the planters' position. They also went on taking temporary leases from the Bettiah Raj. Some villages were settled in perpetuity with factories by the Ramnagar Raj also.

In the settlement report of 1899 it is stated that the indigo concerns exercised the rights of landlords in nearly half of the Champaran district, either as proprietors or tenure-holders, and that the indigo industry owed the strength of its position in the district to the fact that the planters possessed a landlord's interest in so large an area. Not the least noticeable result of this was that as most of their indigo was now grown on land of which they were the landlords, they could dictate exacting terms to petty proprietors and cultivators.

The proportion of land held by the planters as proprietors was inconsiderable, amounting to only half per cent in the whole Champaran district. Generally speaking, the interest of the indigo concerns in the land was mainly of tenure-holders, but in Bettiah, Motihari, Gobindganj and Kessariya, where the proportion of land held on permanent tenure varied from 23 to 45 per cent, it was certainly as secure as a proprietary right.

The cultivation of indigo was more extensive in Champaran than in any other district of Bihar. According to the survey of 1892-97, no less than 21 factories with 48 outworks employing 33,000 labourers had been established in the district, while the area under indigo cultivation was 95,970 acres or about seven per cent of the cultivated area.

The rate of indigo cultivation increased under pressure, but the planters continued to indulge in barbaric methods.

The press continued to comment on the ryots' grievances and the attention of the Government was also drawn to them directly from time to time. In 1875 the Commissioner of Patna proposed that a commission be appointed to inquire into the grievances of the indigo cultivators. The Lieutenant-Governor, Sir Richard Temple, thought the appointment of a commission would lead to agitation, and he accordingly gave orders to district officers to decide disputes between the planters and the tenants in an impartial manner. In 1877 Mr. Stuart Bayley, the Commissioner of Patna, wrote that although the appointment of a commission had been considered inopportune, "the fact remained that there was much discontent manifest enough to local officers".

About this time Sir Richard Temple retired, and Sir Ashley Eden became the Lieutenant-Governor of Bengal. He had been magistrate at the time of indigo disturbances in Bengal and was fully acquainted with the activities of the planters. He thought that instead of taking action openly, it would be better to get the indigo planters to agree to some reforms. He accordingly impressed upon them that the practice of indigo cultivation under the *asamiwar* system was harmful to the interests of the tenants and that they should, therefore, raise the price of indigo, and that good feelings between the tenants and the planters could be restored only if the planters got indigo cultivated on purely business principles. He emphasized the fact that it was not proper for the planters to exact forced labour from their tenants.

The planters knew that in Sir Ashley Eden the ryots had a sympathetic ruler. They united together and established the Bihar Planters' Association in order to resist drastic reforms by giving some minor concessions to the ryots. In its very first meeting, the association decided to enhance the price of indigo cultivation from Rs. 9 to Rs. 10-5-0 per acre. It was also decided that, if any complaint was made against a member of planters' association, the association should be entitled to inquire thereinto and if that member did not obey its orders he would be liable to be removed from the association. There were 73 factories belonging to the association, employing 75,900 persons, exclusive of a large staff, Indian and European, for management and supervision.

From about 1900 the industry began to suffer from the competition of artificial dyes in Europe and from the rise in prices of foodgrains and the consequent demand for land in Bihar. The price of the natural dye fell rapidly from Rs. 232 per factory maund to Rs. 130 in 1912-13. The area under indigo cultivation naturally decreased and the history of the industry merged into the more general history of the relations between the landlords and the tenants. In 1900 the hated system of *tinkathia* prevailed. In the non-indigo concerns the ryots paid to their immediate landlords various *abwabs* with a general incidence of about Rs. 3 per bigha. The indigo concerns, therefore, began to decrease the area under cultivation and to levy compensation from the tenants for releasing them from the obligation of cultivation of indigo under the *tinkathia* system. This coincided with the gradual awakening of the tenantry to the doubtful legality of these additional considerations. Complaints were received but led to no improvement. The bad feeling increased, until widespread disturbances broke out in 1907. The most noteworthy event of this year was the murder of Mr. Bloomfield, manager of Telhara concern, who had refused to sanction the transfer of holdings.

From early in the year 1907 there was a general feeling of uneasiness in the Sathi village situated in the Bettiah subdivision. Meetings of Muslim ryots were held under the guidance of Shaikh Gulab. They refused to grow indigo on the ground that it was unprofitable. The planters insisted on having indigo grown. Convictions were obtained but reversed on appeal. A common fund was raised by the ryots for contesting the cases and petitions were put in against the factory. The factory shut off the supply of water through the *pains* which it had constructed, and there followed thefts of water and prosecutions on this account. In 1908 the ryots disputed with the factory the possession of the oats and other crops grown in the *tinkathia* lands and thousands of cases were instituted. In sympathy, the ryots of a factory situated in the Ramnagar Estate petitioned against their European landlord and complained of illegal exactions. The offshoot of the Sathi dispute was an agreement that whatever crops in the *tinkathia* land were grown from factory seed should be taken by the factory, while the ryots should take the crops grown from seed supplied by themselves, and that such ryots as did not want to grow indigo or oats on the *tinkathia* system should pay for the irrigation from the *pains* at the rate of Rs. 3 for every bigha of their holding instead of at the previous rate of about two annas, and should execute agreements to this effect.

The uneasiness continued through the summer of 1908 and, at the Bettiah mela, a general feeling of dissatisfaction was expressed against the whole *tinkathia* system. Sitalrai took the lead and continued the agitation among the tenants. The peasants' organization was so perfected that, on hearing a particular sound, the tenants of several villages would assemble at a fixed place. In October 1908, certain tenants went into action and attacked a peon and the manager of the Parsa factory. This was followed by violent acts in the Parsa, Mallahia, Bairia and Kundia areas. Military police were rushed to protect the planters. Fifty-seven criminal cases were instituted and 266 people were convicted of acts of violence. Sitalrai was sentenced to thirty months' rigorous imprisonment and a fine of Rs. 1,000. The Government further posted an additional punitive police force in the disturbed area and Rs. 30,000, the cost of maintaining the force, was realized from the tenants.

By November 1908 the tension had eased. Mr. Gourlay, who was then Director of Agriculture and had at one time been Subdivisional Officer in Bettiah, was deputed to make an informal inquiry, which he completed in December and January. His report was submitted in April 1909 and, after informal discussions between the Government and members of the Planters' Association, certain changes were made in the existing system, the chief items being an increase of the price per acre paid for indigo cultivation from Rs. 12 to Rs. 13, and the introduction of a bye-law whereby the area to be taken from the ryot each year was reduced from three *kathas* to two *kathas* in the bigha.

Mr. Gourlay's report was a restatement of all the old grievances which had figured in the previous inquiries. Mr. Gourlay found that the cultivation of indigo on the *asamiwar* system did not pay the ryot, that the ryot had to give up his best land for indigo, that the cultivation required labour which could be more profitably employed elsewhere, and that the system was irksome and led to oppression by the factory servants.

Mr. Gourlay's report was not published because it declared that the tenants' grievances were well-founded and the planters were to blame. The Government released all those tenants who had been convicted and were in prison.

The years 1910 and 1911 were free from incidents. At the end of December 1911, about 15,000 tenants assembled at Narkatiganj railway station to state their grievances to His Majesty the King Emperor, who was then on his way back from Nepal. They shouted out their grievances but, on His Majesty's inquiry, it was represented to him as an expression of welcome and joy on their part. When His Majesty reached Calcutta, the ryots sent representatives to submit a memorial to him. This was forwarded under His Majesty's commands to the Government of India for disposal, but it was returned to the senders in February 1912 for the reason that it had not been submitted through the proper channel. Then several memorials were submitted to the Government, but they were referred to the planters concerned and then filed.

Meanwhile, with the decline of indigo cultivation, the landlord's practice to claim compensation from the tenants for releasing them from the obligation to grow indigo became general. Compensation was levied by two methods. First, in villages held in *mokarri* or permanent lease in which the planter was really in the position of a proprietor, the ryots executed contracts to pay enhanced rents. The enhancements were about sixty per cent over the original rents and were effected by registered documents. This method was known as *sharahbeshi*. Secondly, in villages held on temporary lease, the planter took lump sums called *tawan* from the tenants. There were, of course, exceptions. For instance, the Rajpur concern adopted the *tawan* system in all its villages and the Pipra concern, while enhancing rent in *mokarri* villages, continued *tinkathia* cultivation in the *thikadari* villages. The Lalsaraiya concern adopted neither method but merely assessed rent on excess areas discovered in the possession of the ryots at the last settlement, which the factory had agreed to leave unassessed so long as the ryots continued *tinkathia* cultivation.

These substituted arrangements continued through 1912, 1913 and 1914 and were in full swing when revisional survey and settlement operations started in October 1913. The situation was complicated by the fact that the Bettiah Estate applied for enhancement of rent in all its *thikadari* villages.

In 1914-15 the record of rights for the Bettiah subdivision was attested. Towards the end of 1914 a number of petitions were presented to the Lieutenant-Governor complaining of *abwab* and other matters, which were reported on by the Settlement Department. It was clearly proved that this illegal cess was being collected on a large scale. The Bettiah Estate stopped all such levies by its *thikadars,* but the administration was not in a position to enforce a similar prohibition in the Ramnagar Estate. In 1915-16 the record of the Motihari subdivision was attested. The legality of *sharahbeshi* was strenuously contested by the ryots. In the majority of cases the enhanced rates were allowed, as the ryots had not the means to prove their main plea, which was that force had been used to procure the new agreements.

Some of the planters realized as much as Rs. 50,000 per year from enhancement of rates in their *mokarri* villages. The ryots continued to send petitions to the Government stating that they were being forced to agree to enhancements. One of such petitions was submitted by Lomrajsingh to the Commissioner of Tirhut in 1914. The petition was signed by 700 tenants. As a result Mr. Norman, the manager of the Peepra factory, prosecuted Lomrajsingh and fourteen others for defamation. Mr. Beal, the magistrate, convicted them and sentenced them to six months' imprisonment and a fine of Rs. 24,000. On appeal to the District Judge, Mr. A. E. Scroope, all the accused were acquitted. In the course of his judgement, Mr. Scroope said:

"For the appellants the contention is that the wholesale execution of *kabulyats* was brought about by nothing less than an organized system of oppression by the factory servants, hangers-on and *umidwars* who represent the factory in the eyes of the ordinary ryot, and that the chief means resorted to were (1) stoppage of cultivation till the *kabulyats* were executed, (2) bringing in women to register, whose husbands or male representatives had been away to avoid registering, and (3) criminal cases. Again, looking to the probabilities, there is no doubt that whilst the intentions of a manager may be one thing, the acts of the factory servants may be, and often are, quite another. It was undoubtedly to the interest of the factory to substitute these new agreements for the obligation to grow indigo. This being so, it is by no means improbable that the factory servants would put pressure on the ryots to come in and execute *kabulyats*. . .Anyhow, taking the evidence as it stands, it is impossible to avoid the conclusion that stoppage of cultivation was used by the factory as a means of getting these *kabulyats* executed, and this certainly justified a representation to the Commissioner, as it is hard to imagine a more unfair stimulus to execute a document, and the adjectives used in the petition to the Commissioner are not unreasonable epithets to apply to it. . . Then, as regards the allegations about women, the defence puts in *kabulyats,* all of which, it is denied by the prosecution, were filed up first in a man's name and eventually registered by a woman. Certainly the factory's action in these instances may have been perfectly bona fide, but the necessity has not been explained for this urgency and for not waiting till the men had made their periodic returns."

The planters were well organized and ruthlessly exploited the helpless, ignorant ryots with the active help of some of the highly placed officials. With the help of the Anglo-Indian press and powerful business connections, they had a direct access to the Viceroy and the Secretary of State. When Lord Hardinge visited Patna in 1913, the planters presented an address to him, in reply to which he gave them a certificate of good behaviour: "Today, as far as I know, the relations between the Bihar planters and their ryots are cordial and satisfactory in the North Bihar districts."

In reply to this, Babu Brajkishore Prasad, in his presidential address at the Bihar Provincial Conference of 1914, said :

"The highest officials in the land have utilized their replies to the addresses of welcome from the planting community to bestow upon them glowing panegyrics on the valuable services they are said to have rendered to Tirhut. I do not grudge the planters these eulogiums and I wish them joy. But I do maintain that there is another side of the shield and, whatever good the planters might have done, their dealings with the ryots have brought about a serious agrarian situation and they have resulted in considerable suffering and misery to the poor and defenceless villagers. It is well known that the ryots' allegations against the planters, which have been held by courts to be generally well-founded, are to the effect that they are found to execute illegal *sattas* by methods of coercion, including the institution of vexatious cases, that fines and cesses are unlawfully realized from them and they are ill-treated if they attempt in the least to refuse compliance with the orders of the planters. So far as the execution of the *sattas* is concerned, it is strange that registration offices are opened at factories to suit the convenience of the planters. These allegations are serious enough in all conscience to merit a thorough and sifting inquiry in the interest not only of the ryots but of the planters as well. In my opinion the Government will be well advised if, far from blinking so serious a problem, they tackle it in the only way possible, namely, by appointing a small mixed committee of qualified officials and non-officials to thoroughly investigate the matter by means of an open inquiry and by acting upon its recommendations. Otherwise, I may warn the Government that there are rocks ahead and they had better look out."

Again in 1915 the Bihar Provincial Conference passed a resolution demanding an inquiry committee to examine the ryots' grievances. Rajkumar Shukla, a representative of the tenants, described graphically at the conference the plight of the ryots. The Legislative Council met in May and Brajkishore Prasad proposed the following resolution:

"That this Council recommends to the Lieutenant-Governor-in-Council that a committee of qualified officials and non-officials be appointed to make an immediate and searching inquiry into the case of strained relations between the planters and ryots in the district of Champaran and to suggest remedies therefor."

The Government of Sir Charles Bayley did not accept this resolution. In reply it was said that the Government from time to time had inquiries made by local officers and at the time the survey and settlement of the district was going on, and whatever grievances the tenants might have would be placed before the Settlement Officer whose report would doubtless be authoritative.

Babu Brajkishore Prasad was requested to withdraw the resolution. He only said in reply that if the Government gave a pledge to publish the report of the inquiry which was then alleged to be made by the Settlement Officer, he might withdraw his resolution. The Government did not even agree to this.

CHAMPARAN

MR. J. A. SWEENEY, the Settlement Officer, submitted his report in June 1915. The complaints of the tenants of Champaran were found by him to be mostly true. The incidence of the illegal cess, *abwab*, was equal to the legal rent and thus every tenant had to pay double the amount he was legally liable to pay. Under the Bengal Tenancy Act a person who realized *abwab* was liable to pay double the amount realized by him as penalty. No steps, however, were taken to enforce the law even against such planters as admitted having realized an illegal cess.

There were no less than forty types of *abwabs* in addition to the fines which were exacted by the planters from the ryots. For water supplied by the planter the ryot had to pay *painkharcha*. Canal or *pain*, in some cases, did not even exist, but the ryot was made to pay Rs. 3 per bigha of land. In other cases the upkeep of the canal did not cost even Rs. 300 but by way of cess Rs. 9,000 was realized every year. There were instances of *painkharcha* being realized in lump sums too. In six types of *abwabs* the ryot had to pay Rs. 3 per bigha over and above the rent : *painkharcha*, *salami*, *tinkathia*, *lagan*, *bandhbehri*, *bethmati*. When a tenant died, his heir had to pay *bapahi-putahi*, a sort of death duty. At the time of the marriage of a tenant's son or daughter a tax of Rs. 1-4-0 called *marwach* was realized by the planter. At the time of the marriage of a widow, *sagaura* of Rs. 5 was collected. Four types of cesses—*dawatpuja*, *phaguahi*, *dasahari*, *chaitnawami*—were realized by the planters on the occasion of Hindu festivals. When the planters wanted to purchase elephants for shikar, the tenants had to raise money from among themselves and it was called *hathiahi*. Similar taxes were collected from the tenants for purchasing a horse, a motor-car or a boat, namely, *ghorahi*, *motorahi* and *hawahi*. If the planter fell ill, the tenants had to pay for his treatment ; it was called *ghawahi*. *Rasidawan* was paid to the village officer at the rate of one anna per receipt he issued for rent realized from the tenants. There were four more such taxes, under different names, serving the same purpose. The *abwabs* make a formidable list.

Mr. Amman, manager of the Belwa factory, said openly: "Is the *thikadar* to blame for collecting these *abwabs*, for the *thikadar* is paid to squeeze and must squeeze to pay ?"

As regards the *abwab*, the Settlement Officer gave his verdict in favour of the tenants, but in respect of the enhancement agreements he sided with the planters. The tenants stated that the enhancement agreements were imposed on them, but the Settlement Officer decided that coercion was not proved. Even where it was established that the agreements for enhancement were taken under undue influence or coercion and consequently invalid, the Settlement Officer recorded in the record of rights of the tenants that they were under an obligation to grow indigo in three *kathas* of every bigha of their holding. They hated *tinkathia* system and preferred to pay enhanced rates. They had built high hopes to get relief from the Settlement Officer, but they were sorely disappointed.

The war broke out in 1914 and the prices of all commodities soared high. With the supplies of synthetic dyes from Germany cut off, such natural dyes as were still obtainable, of which the indigo was the most important, found a ready market. The quantity of export of the dye rose from 142,000 lbs. just before the war and 600,000 lbs. in 1914-15 to about one and a half million pounds in 1916-17. Planters made fortunes, whereas the ryots had to buy all their requirements at enhanced prices.

Rajkumar Shukla was one of those agriculturists who had been under this harrow, and he was filled with a passion to wash away the stain of indigo for the thousands who were suffering as he had suffered. He gave vent to the grievances of the tenants from the platform of the Bihar Provincial Conference held in 1915 at Chapra. In December 1916 he proceeded to Lucknow to acquaint the Indian National Congress with the plight of the indigo workers in Bihar.

The Lucknow session of the Congress was a momentous one and was attended by over 2,300 delegates and a large number of visitors from all over the country. The year 1916 had been a period of marked political activity in India under the leadership of Tilak, Mrs. Besant and Jinnah. The results of this activity were epitomized in the proceedings of the Congress and the Muslim League, meetings of which were held simultaneously. After the split at Surat, Tilak for the first time attended the Congress at Lucknow with a number of followers. Along with other provinces Bihar was represented by a large contingent of delegates, including Brajkishore Prasad and Rajendra Prasad. Among those distinguished leaders present at the session were Mrs. Besant, Malaviya, Surendranath Banerjea, Jinnah and Mazharul Haq. Gandhi was there but he was not prominent in the political arena. Tilak was the most dominating figure in the country and was looked upon as a hero by all.

Raikumar Shukla approached Lokamanya Tilak and Malaviya with the grievances of indigo cultivators but they told him that the immediate question before the Congress was political freedom. The simple cultivator was impatient with regard to his own pressing problems He had heard Gandhi's name as a saviour of indentured labourers in South Africa. Gandhi was dressed like a Kathiawadi peasant and did not wear even shoes, as a sign of mourning over Gokhale's death. He lived in the delegates' camps not far from the Bihar delegates. Raikumar Shukla brought Babu Brajkishore Prasad to Gandhi's tent and touched Gandhi's feet with a request to move a resolution on the plight of the Champaran ryots. Brajkishore Babu was dressed in a black alpaca *achkkan* and trousers. Gandhi thought that he must be a vakil exploiting the simple agriculturists. Having patiently heard from him something of Champaran, Gandhi firmly replied : "I can give no opinion without seeing the condition with my own eyes. You will please move the resolution in the Congress, but leave me free for the present."

On the second day of the Congress session the following resolution on Champaran was moved by Brajkishore Prasad : "The Congress most respectfully urges on the Government the desirability of appointing a mixed committee of officials and non-officals to inquire into the causes of agrarian trouble and the strained relations between the indigo ryots and European planters in North Bihar and to suggest remedies therefor."

Rajkumar Shukla, a representative of the tenants, made a speech from the Congress platform, supporting the resolution. He was glad but far from satisfied. He wanted Gandhi personally to visit Champaran and witness the miseries of the ryots there. He and his colleagues had previously written a letter to Gandhi at his Ahmedabad address. He then had no time, as he was campaigning for the abolition of the indenture system. After the resolution was passed in the Congress, the Bihar delegates along with Rajkumar Shukla approached Gandhi and pressed him to visit Bihar. He promised that he would try to spend a few days in Bihar in March or April of the following year.

From Lucknow Gandhi went to Cawnpore. Rajkumar Shukla followed him there. He insisted : "Champaran is very near here. Please give a day." Gandhi further committed himself by saying: "Pray excuse me this time. But I promise that I will come."

Gandhi returned to the Sabarmati ashram. Rajkumar Shukla was there too. "Pray fix the day now," he said. "Well," replied Gandhi, "I have to be in Calcutta in March, come and meet me then, and take me from there." He did not know where he was to go, what to do and what things to see.

Rajkumar Shukla, on behalf of the tenants, wrote a letter to Gandhi on February 27, 1917. Gandhi wrote in reply that he would be in Calcutta on March 7 and inquired where Rajkumar Shukla could meet him. The letter did not reach him till after the 7th. He had, however, heard that Gandhi had gone to Calcutta but on arriving there he learnt that he had already left for Delhi. Rajkumar Shukla returned to Champaran and again wrote to Gandhi and received a reply on March 16, saying that he would take the earliest opportunity of visiting Champaran. On April 3 Gandhi sent a telegram to Rajkumar Shukla that he was going to Calcutta where he would stay with Bhupendranath Basu and asked Rajkumar Shukla to meet him there. Before Gandhi reached Bhupen Babu's place, Rajkumar Shukla had gone and established himself there. Thus this ignorant, unsophisticated but resolute agriculturist captured him.

No one knew about Gandhi's proposed visit and although some of the delegates from Bihar were present in Calcutta at the All-India Congress Committee's meeting, no one had any talk with him regarding Champaran.

On April 7, Gandhi accompanied by Rajkumar Shukla, left Calcutta for Champaran. The two looked like fellow rustics.

Gandhi had seen packets of indigo, but little dreamed that it was grown and manufactured in Champaran at great hardships to thousands of agriculturists. He had not known even the name, much less the geographical position, of Champaran, and had hardly any notion of indigo plantations.

Champaran district is situated in the north-western corner of Bihar. The biggest river in the district is the Gandak, which in the olden times flowed through the middle of the district. It has changed its course but the traces of its old course arc still there in the shape of forty-three lakes in the district. Many of these are deep but their water is not drinkable. It is used in indigo factories many of which have been constructed on the banks of these lakes.

There are only two towns in Champaran—Motihari, which is the headquarters of the district, and Bettiah—and 2,841 villages. Of its population of two million, 98 per cent inhabit the rural areas. Like other districts of Bihar there is preponderance of Hindus in Champaran. Bhojpuri, a dialect of Hindi, is spoken by both Hindus and Muslims.

Champaran or Champaranya is associated with great historic events since centuries. Its thick jungles served as the place of retreat, *tapovana*, of rishis. Dhruva was born in this forest and did his penance here. This was the land of King Janaka. The ashram of Valmiki was also situated here. Buddha passed through Champaran on his last march from Vaisali to Kusinar. Three or four pillars erected by Asoka still stand here as a witness to the historic and cultural importance of Champaran. The Lichchhavis and Gupta kings, Asoka and Harsha-vardhana, are intimately associated with this ancient land.

From such glorious past Champaran sank steadily into an era of white planters' rule of loot and slavery. Gandhi's mission was to wash away the stain of indigo and end the slavery.

On the way to Champaran, Gandhi arrived in Patna on the morning of April 10. This was his first visit to the city. He had no friend there with whom he could think of putting up. He had an idea that Rajkumar Shukla must have some influence in Patna. He had come to know him a little more on the journey, and on reaching Patna Gandhi had no illusions left concerning him. "He was perfectly innocent of everything. The vakils that he had taken to be his friends were really nothing of the sort. Rajkumar was more or less a menial to them. Between such agriculturist clients and their vakils there is a gulf as wide as the Ganges in flood."

Rajkumar Shukla took him to Babu Rajendra Prasad's house in Patna. Rajendra Babu had gone to Puri. There was only a servant in the house, who paid no attention to the guests. Gandhi had with him something to eat. He wanted dates which Rajkumar procured for him from the bazar. There was strict untouchability in Bihar. Gandhi has related this unhappy experience in his autobiography :

"I might not draw water at the well whilst the servants were using it, lest drops of water from my bucket might pollute them, the servants not knowing to what caste I belonged. Rajkumar directed me to the indoor latrine, the servant promptly directed me to the outdoor one. All this was far from surprising or irritating to me, for I was inured to such things. The servants were doing the duty, which they thought Rajendra Babu would wish them to do.

"These entertaining experiences enhanced my regard, if they also enabled me to know him better. I saw now that Rajkumar could not guide me, and that I must take the reins in my own hand."

Gandhi knew Mazharul Haq in London when he was studying for the bar, and when he met him in the Bombay Congress in 1915, the year in which Mazharul Haq was President of the Muslim League, he had renewed the acquaintance, and extended Gandhi an invitation to stay with him whenever he happened to go to Patna. Gandhi bethought himself of this invitation and sent him a note indicating the purpose of his visit. Mazharul Haq immediately came in his car, and pressed him to accept his hospitality. Gandhi thanked him and requested him to guide him to his destination by the first available train, the railway guide being useless to an utter stranger like him. Mazharul Haq suggested that he should first go to Muzaffarpur, the headquarters of the Commissioner of Tirhut division as well as of the Bihar Planters' Association. There was a train for that place the same evening, and Mazharul Haq sent Gandhi off by it. J. B. Kripalani, who was then a professor in the Muzaffarpur College, was telegraphically informed of his arrival.

The train reached Muzaffarpur at midnight. Kripalani had never met Gandhi before, although they had corresponded with each other. Kripalani accompanied by a crowd of students was waiting at the station to receive Gandhi, but they could not recognize him. Gandhi was walking barefoot, wearing a coarse dhoti, a kurta and a cap, carrying a small bundle tucked under his arm and a small tiffin-box, containing some dry fruit, in one of his hands. Rajkumar Shukla with pride introduced Gandhi to the crowd. The students gave a reception at the station, honoured him by waving an earthen oil-lamp, and dragged his carriage. Kripalani had just resigned his post and had no rooms of his own. He was staying with Professor Malkani, who, therefore, virtually became Gandhi's host. It was an extraordinary thing in those days for a Government servant to harbour a man like Gandhi.

Kripalani, that night, spoke to him about the desperate condition of Bihar, particularly of the Tirhut division. In the morning a small group of vakils called on him. One of them was Ramnavmi Prasad whose earnestness appealed to Gandhi. "It is not possible," said Ramnavmi Prasad, "for you to do the kind of work you have come for, if you stay in Professor Malkani's quarters. You must come and stay with one of us. Gaya Babu is a well-known vakil here. I have come on his behalf to invite you to stay with him. I confess we are all afraid of the Government, but we shall render what help we can. Most of the things Rajkumar Shukla has told you are true. It is a pity that our leaders are not here today. I have, however, wired to them both, Babu Brajkishore Prasad and Babu Rajendra Prasad. I expect them to arrive shortly, and they are sure to be able to give you all the information you want and to help you considerably. Pray come over to Gaya Babu's place."

This was a request that Gandhi could not resist, though he hesitated for fear of embarrassing Gaya Babu. But he put him at ease, and so he went over to stay with him.

Brajkishore Babu now arrived from Darbhanga and Rajendra Babu from Puri. Brajkishore Babu was not the Babu Brajkishore Prasad that Gandhi had met in Lucknow. Brajkishore impressed him this time with his "humility, simplicity, goodness and extraordinary faith, so characteristic of the Biharis", and Gandhi s heart was joyous over it. He felt himself becoming bound to this circle of colleagues in life-long friendship.

Brajkishore Babu acquainted him with the facts of the case. He used to be in the habit of taking up the cases of the poor tenants. When he won any such case, he had the consolation that he was doing something for these poor people. Not that he did not charge fees from these simple peasants.

"Lawyers labour under the belief that, if they do not charge the fees, they will have no wherewithal to run their households, and will not be able to render effective help to the poor people. The figures of the fees they charged and the standard of a barrister s fees in Bengal and Bihar, staggered me," observed Gandhi. We gave Rs. 10,000 to so and so for his opinion,' I was told. Nothing less than four figures in any case." The Bihari vakils listened to his kindly reproach and did not misunderstand him.

"Having studied these cases," said Gandhi, "I have come to the conclusion that we should stop going to law courts. Taking such cases to the courts does little good. Where the ryots are so crushed and fear-stricken, law courts are useless. The real relief for them is to be free from fear. We cannot sit still until we have driven *tinkathia* out of Bihar. I had thought that I should be able to leave here in two days, but I now realize that the work might take even two years. I am prepared to give that time, if necessary. I am now feeling my ground, but I want your help."

Babu Brajkishore Prasad, a cool-headed vakil, said quietly : "We shall render all the help we can, but pray tell us what kind of help you will need."

"I shall have little use for your legal knowledge," Gandhi replied. "I want clerical assistance and help in interpretation. It may be necessary to face imprisonment, but, much as I would love you to run that risk, you would go only so far as you feel yourselves capable of going. Even turning yourselves into clerks and giving up your profession for an indefinite period is no small thing. I find it difficult to understand Bhojpuri, the local dialect of Hindi, and I shall not be able to read papers written in Kaithi or Urdu. I shall want you to translate them for me. We cannot afford to pay for this work. It should all be done for love and out of a spirit of service."

Brajkishore Prasad understood this immediately, and now cross-examined Gandhi and his own companions by turn. He then tried to ascertain the implications of all that Gandhi had said,—how long their service would be required, how many of them would be needed, whether they might serve by turns and so on. Then he asked the vakils how far they were prepared for sacrifice. Ultimately they gave Gandhi this assurance : "Such and such a number of us will do whatever you may ask. Some of us will be with you for as much time as you may require. The idea of accommodating ourselves to imprisonment is a novel thing for us. We will try to adjust ourselves to it."

Gandhi's object was to inquire into the condition of the Champaran ryots and understand their grievances against the indigo planters. For this purpose it was necessary that he should meet thousands of the ryots. But he deemed it essential, before starting on his inquiry, to know the planters' side of the case and see the Commissioner of Tirhut division. He sought and was granted appointments by both.

On April 11 Gandhi met Mr. J. M. Wilson, the secretary of the Bihar Planters' Association. Mr. Wilson told him plainly that he had no business to come between the planters and their tenants, but if he had any representation to make, he might submit it in writing. Gandhi politely replied that he did not regard himself as an outsider, and that he had every right to inquire into the condition of the tenants if they desired him to do so. Mr. Wilson said that if Gandhi commenced this work during war-time, the self-seeking agitators would utilize the opportunity for their selfish ends which might do more harm than good to those to help whom he came.

Two days later, Gandhi interviewed Mr. L. F. Morshead, the Commissioner of Tirhut division. The Commissioner proceeded to bully him, expressed his disapproval of his visit to Bihar and inquired who had brought him there. He added that an inquiry was being made on behalf of the Government and that he would not give any assistance to him in his inquiry and advised him forthwith to leave Tirhut. Gandhi told him that he had been receiving letters from the people for a long time, but he could not produce them before him ; that at the Lucknow Congress the delegates from Bihar had asked him to move a resolution on the Champaran problem but that he had refused to do so on the ground that he would not make himself a party to it unless he had seen things with his own eyes ; and that, therefore, the delegates had asked him to visit Champaran and he was accordingly there.

He acquainted his co-workers with the Commissioner's attitude, and warned them that there was every likelihood of the Government stopping him from proceeding further, and that he might have to go to jail earlier than he expected, and that, if he was to be arrested, it would be best that the arrest should take place in Motihari or if possible in Bettiah. It was advisable, therefore, that he should go to those places as early as possible. Rajkumar Shukla's place was in the vicinity of Bettiah, and the tenants in its neighbourhood were the poorest in the district. Rajkumar Shukla wanted Gandhi to see them and he was also anxious to do so.

The news of Gandhi's arrival had already spread and a number of tenants came all the way to Muzaffarpur. Gandhi listened to their grievances and perused such papers as he could get. He had not up to this time formed any idea as to the true situation in Champaran, and at times used to ask : "Is it possible ? Can this be true ?"

Gandhi's resolve to proceed to Champaran became firmer. He asked prominent Bihari delegates to the Lucknow Congress to give him a letter to the effect that they had requested him during the Congress session in 1916 to hold an inquiry in Champaran. Along with this letter he sent a letter of his own to the Commissioner of Tirhut division, stating that he had come to find the truth with regard to the relation between the planters and the ryots in view of certain statements which had been made to him. That was the only object of his visit and all that he wanted was peace with honour.

On April 14 he decided to start for Champaran on the following day. In the evening he visited a neighbouring village. He entered the huts of the poor, saw how they lived and talked to children and women. He told his colleagues that as long as the condition of the villages was not improved, India could not be happy.

After returning from the village, he talked to his colleagues. He related to them his experiences in South Africa : how when one worker was jailed, others used to take his place and how when he was also removed, his place was taken by another and so on. He added : "I wish that work should be done in the same way here. I know that the officials and the planters would act harshly towards me and a warrant for my arrest may come any moment. I am, therefore, anxious to reach Champaran as quickly as possible, so that whatever action they may have to take against me, may be taken in the midst of the ryots of Champaran. I know that in Bihar I cannot get men of this type ; those who will accompany me will do so only as clerks and interpreters ; as for the rest, we shall see later."

Gandhi started for Motihari on Sunday, April 15, by the midday train. He was accompanied by two lawyers, Babu Dharnidhar and Babu Ramnavmi Prasad, who acted as his interpreters. As he was expecting a warrant of arrest at any moment, he carried on his person only a few necessary articles and the rest of the things were kept in a small trunk separately. He was seen off at the Muzaffarpur station by a number of people and on the way, at every station, a large crowd of peasants greeted him enthusiastically.

Gandhi reached Motihari at three in the afternoon and went straight to Gorakh Prasad, a pleader, in whose small bungalow he stayed. The very same day he got the news that in a near-by village, Jasaulipatti, a tenant was severely beaten and his property was destroyed. Gandhi decided to visit the village the next morning.

On April 16, at nine in the morning, Gandhi and his interpreter Dharnidhar Prasad, started for Jasaulipatti on elephant's back, the common mode of conveyance in Bihar villages. Gandhi was not used to riding an elephant. A hot dusty wind added to the inconvenience. But he was too engrossed in the problems to think of discomfort. Among the subjects discussed by him with his companion was also the custom of purdah in Bihar. "It is not my desire that our women should adopt the western mode of living," he said, "but we must realize what harm this pernicious system of purdah does to their health and in how many ways they are deprived of the privilege of helping their husbands."

By noon they had travelled about nine miles from Motihari and reached a village called Chandrahia. Gandhi decided to stop there for a while and see the condition of the village, which happened to belong to the Motihari factory. The majority of its residents were labourers and they had gone to the factory for work. A solitary man whom they met in the village said that even the collector dared not do anything against the sahib, the manager of the factory. While this conversation was going on, a man in plain clothes was seen coming on a bicycle. He was a Police Sub-Inspector. He approached Gandhi and told him that the superintendent had sent his *salams*. Gandhi saw what he meant. He was expecting that something of this sort would happen. "You need not mind it," he told Dharnidhar Babu, "you proceed to Jasaulipatti and do the work there."

Gandhi got into a bullock cart which the sub-inspector had hired. After a while, an *ekka* was engaged by the sub-inspector ; at his request Gandhi left the cart and got into the *ekka*. When they had covered a short distance, a Deputy Superintendent of Police came in a tandem and requested Gandhi to leave the *ekka* and get into the tandem. When they had gone a little further, the officer stopped the tandem, showed a notice to Gandhi and drove him to his place in Motihari.

The notice, dated April 16, 1917, signed by the District Magistrate, Mr. W. B. Heycock, addressed to "Mr. M. K. Gandhi, at present in Motihari," read as follows :

"Whereas it has been made to appear to me from the letter of the Commissioner of the Division, a copy of which is attached to this order, that your presence in any part of the district will endanger the public peace and may lead to serious disturbance which may be accompanied by loss of life and whereas urgency is of the utmost importance; now, therefore, I do hereby order you to abstain from remaining in the district, which you are required to leave by the next available train."

The Commissioner's note addressed to the District Magistrate of Champaran said :

"Mr. M. K. Gandhi has come here in response to what he describes as an insistent public demand to inquire into the conditions under which Indians work on indigo plantations and desires the help of the local administration. He came to see me this morning and, I explained that the relations between the planters and the ryots had engaged the attention of the administration since the sixties, and that we were particularly concerned with a phase of the problem in Champaran now ; but that it was doubtful whether the intervention of a stranger in the middle of the treatment of our case would not prove an embarrassment. I indicated the potentialities of disturbance in Champaran, asked for credentials to show an insistent demand for his inquiry and said that the matter would probably need reference to the Government.

"I expected that Mr. Gandhi would communicate with me again before he proceeds to Champaran but I have been informed since our interview that his object is likely to be agitation rather than a genuine search for knowledge and it is possible that he may proceed without further reference. I consider that there is a danger of disturbance to the public tranquillity should he visit your district. I have the honour to request you to direct him by an order under section 144 Cr. P. C. to leave it at once if he should appear."

When Gandhi was asked to acknowledge the service of the notice, he wrote to the magistrate that he did not propose to comply with it and leave Champaran till his inquiry was finished :

"With reference to the order under section 144 of the Criminal Procedure Code just served upon me, I beg to state that I am sorry that you have felt called upon to issue it and I am sorry that the Commissioner of the division has totally misinterpreted my position. Out of a sense of public responsibility I felt it to be my duty to say that I am unable to leave this district but if it so pleases the authorities, I shall submit to the order suffering the penalty of disobedience.

"I must emphatically repudiate the Commissioner's suggestion that my object is likely to be agitation. My desire is purely and simply for a genuine search for knowledge. And this I shall continue to satisfy so long as I am left free."

Pandit Malaviya, Mazharul Haq and other Indian leaders were informed telegraphically about the latest development in Champaran and Mr. Andrews was wired to come at once. Gandhi kept awake the whole night writing letters and giving necessary instructions to Brajkishore Prasad. He also prepared a detailed programme of work to be followed after his imprisonment.

ON TRIAL

On April 17, 1917 the work of recording the statements of cultivators began in the small compound of Gandhi's residence. A police officer arrived on the scene and started to note down the names of the tenants who gave statements at first stealthily and then openly. The tenants had come in such large numbers that those who recorded the statements had to work the whole day without any rest.

Gandhi's arrest was expected any moment. Telegrams of solidarity were pouring in from all parts of India, offering active co-operation. Mazharul Haq intimated his readiness to start, but was informed that his presence would be necessary after Gandhi's imprisonment. Pandit Malaviya wired for information and expressed his willingness to come, leaving the Hindu University work. Gandhi replied that his presence was not yet needed. Mr. Polak wired that he had already started. Babu Rajendra Prasad was told to come at once with volunteers. When no summons were received up to the evening of the 17th, Gandhi wrote a letter to the district magistrate saying that he intended to visit the neighbouring villages shortly :

"As I have no desire to do anything without the knowledge of the authorities, I beg to inform you that (assuming there is no service of summons for appearance before the court tomorrow) I am going to Shampur and the surrounding villages tomorrow morning. The party hopes to start about 3 a.m.

"I observed yesterday that a police officer followed the party all the way. I may state that we court the fullest publicity and, therefore, beg on my own behalf and that of my colleagues to say that we shall welcome the presence, if we may not have the assistance, of the police in the course of our mission."

On receipt of the letter the district magistrate Mr. Heycock wrote a letter to Gandhi saying that he would be charged with an offence under section 188 of the Indian Penal Code, that a summons would be issued against him, and that he would not leave Motihari.

Gandhi replied, "I shall gladly remain in Motihari tomorrow and await summons." The summons was received calling upon Gandhi to appear before the subdivisional officer on April 18, at 12.30 p. m.

Gandhi went on working the whole night and prepared a statement to be read before the court. He also wrote letters to the secretary of the Planters' Association and the Commissioner of Tirhut in which he recounted the grievances of the tenants and suggested certain remedies. He also wrote a letter to Lord Chelmsford, the Viceroy, describing the latest developments. He recalled his long-standing association with the Government and his record of public service, for which the Kaisar-I-Hind medal had been conferred on him, and said that, while he considered that as a great honour, he felt that since the Government did not trust him enough to let him do public service in Champaran, it would not be proper for him to keep that medal. Accordingly he was asking those with whom he had deposited it to return it to the Viceroy.

He wrote letters to many friends, including Pandit Malaviya, Mazharul Haq and Mr. Polak. He then made copies of his telegrams, letters and the statement. He gave instructions that some of the letters should be posted only after his imprisonment.

After midnight Babu Dharnidhar and Babu Ramnavmi returned from the village, where they had been deputed for the investigation, and made their report to Gandhi. Gandhi, in his turn, told them what had happened since he parted from them. He said that he was standing his trial the following day which would probably end in his going to jail, and wanted to know their plans thereafter.

Dharnidhar replied : "You brought us here to act as interpreters. After your imprisonment, we shall not be needed for that job. We shall, therefore, return to our respective places."

Gandhi asked, "And will you abandon these poor ryots to their fate ?"

Dharnidhar Babu said : "But if you desire, we shall, as long as we can, continue the investigation into their complaints, as you proposed to do. If, however, the Government serve notices on us, directing us to leave the district, as they have done in your case, we shall not disobey that order but quietly depart and send our friends to carry on the work."

Gandhi was not quite pleased with the reply. "Very well, carry on as long as you can," he said.

The night had almost come to an end.

The 18th of April 1917 was a red-letter day for the ryots of

Champaran. The news of the notice and the summons spread like wild fire and Motihari that day witnessed unprecedented scenes. Gorakh Babu's bungalow and the court house overflowed with men. Gandhi had finished all his work during the night and so he was able to cope with crowds. Overwhelmed with the ryots' affection, he wrote in his autobiography :

"A sort of friendliness sprang up between the officials—Collector, Magistrate, Police Superintendent—and myself. I might have legally resisted the notices served on me. Instead I accepted them all, and my conduct towards the officials was correct. They thus saw that I did not want to offend them personally, but that I wanted to offer civil resistance to their orders. In this way they were put at ease, and instead of harassing me they gladly availed themselves of my and co-workers' co-operation in regulating the crowds. But it was an ocular demonstration to them of the fact that their authority was shaken. The people had for the moment lost fear of punishment and yielded obedience to the power of love which their new friend exercised.

"It should be remembered that no one knew me in Champaran. The peasants were all ignorant. Champaran, being far up north of the Ganges, and right at the foot of the Himalayas in close proximity to Nepal, was cut off from the rest of India. The Congress was practically unknown in those parts. Even those who had heard the name of the Congress shrank from joining it or even mentioning it. And now the Congress and its members had entered this land, though not in the name of the Congress, yet in a far more real sense.

"In consultation with my co-workers I had decided that nothing should be done in the name of the Congress. What we wanted was work and not name, substance and not shadow. For the name of the Congress was the *bete noire* of the Government and their controllers—the planters. To them the Congress was a byword for lawyers' wrangles, evasion of law through loopholes, a byword for bomb and anarchical crime and for diplomacy and hypocrisy. We had to disillusion them both. Therefore, we had decided not to mention the name of the Congress and not to acquaint the peasants with the organization called the Congress. It was enough, we thought, if they understood and followed the spirit of the Congress instead of its letter.

"No emissaries had, therefore, been sent there, openly or secretly, on behalf of the Congress to prepare the ground for our arrival.

Rajkumar Shukla was incapable of reaching the thousands of peasants. No political work had yet been done amongst them. The world outside Champaran was not known to them. And yet they received me as though we had been age-long friends. It is no exaggeration, but the literal truth, to say that in this meeting with the peasants I was face to face with God, Ahimsa and Truth.

"When I come to examine my title to this realization, I find nothing but my love for the people. And this in turn is nothing but an expression of my unshakable faith in Ahimsa.

"That day in Champaran was an unforgettable event in my life and a red-letter day for the peasants and for me.

"According to the law I was to be on my trial, but truly speaking Government was to be on its trial. The Commissioner only succeeded in trapping Government in the net which he had spread for me."

On April 18, at 12 noon, the work of recording statements stopped and the tenants were told that the work would again commence on the following day. Gandhi separated those of his things which he wanted to take with himself to jail from those which he wanted to leave behind. At quarter past twelve Gandhi accompanied by Babu Ramnavmi and Babu Dharnidhar started in a carriage for the court. On the way the companions told him that they had decided to follow him in jail, even though others might not. Gandhi exclaimed, "Now I know we shall succeed."

Hundreds of tenants had assembled in the court compound from ten o'clock. When Gandhi entered the courtroom, he was followed by 2,000 men who, in their anxiety to get in, broke the glass panes of the doors. The magistrate seeing the huge crowd asked Gandhi to wait for a little while in mokhtiars' library, and sent for armed police to stop the people from entering the courtroom and to prevent any disturbance in his work. Then Gandhi was called in the courtroom. "Have you got any pleader?" asked the magistrate. "No, none," replied Gandhi.

The Government pleader opened the case and stated that under orders issued under section 144 Cr. P. C. Gandhi ought to have left Champaran on the night of April 16, but that he had not yet done so and he was consequently charged with an offence under section 188 Indian Penal Code.

Gandhi said that on receipt of the order he had sent a reply to the magistrate in which he had stated his reasons for disobeying the order and he wished that the letter should be placed on record.

The trial began. The Government pleader, the magistrate and other officials were on tenterhooks. They were at a loss to know what to do. The Government pleader was pressing the magistrate to postpone the case. But Gandhi interfered and requested the magistrate not to postpone the case, as he wanted to plead guilty to having disobeyed the order to leave Champaran, and read a brief statement :

"With the permission of the court I would like to make a brief statement showing why I have taken a very serious step of seemingly disobeying the order passed under section 144 Criminal Procedure Code. In my humble opinion it is a question of difference of opinion between the local administration and myself. I have entered the country with motives of rendering humanitarian and national service. I have done so in response to a pressing invitation to come and help the ryots, who urge that they are not being fairly treated by indigo planters. I could not render any help without studying the problem. I have, therefore, come to study it with the assistance, if possible, of the administration and the planters. I have no other motive, and cannot believe that my coming can in any way disturb public peace and cause loss of life. I claim to have considerable experience in such matters. The administration, however, have thought differently. I fully appreciate their difficulty, and I admit too that they can only proceed upon information they received. As a law-abiding citizen my first instinct would be, as it was, to obey the order served upon me. But I could not do so without doing violence to my sense of duty to those for whom I have come. I feel that I could just now serve them only by remaining in their midst. I could not, therefore, voluntarily retire. Amid this conflict of duties I could only throw the responsibility of removing me from them on the administration. I am fully conscious of the fact that a person, holding, in the public life of India, a position such as I do, has to be most careful in setting an example. It is my firm belief that in the complex constitution under which we are living, the only safe and honourable course for a self-respecting man is, in the circumstances such as face me, to do what I have decided to do, that is, to submit without protest to the penalty of disobedience.

"I venture to make this statement not in any way in extenuation of the penalty to be awarded against me, but to show that I have disregarded the order served upon me not for want of respect for lawful authority, but in obedience to the higher law of our being, the voice of conscience."

The magistrate repeatedly asked Gandhi, if he pleaded guilty. Gandhi replied, "I have said whatever I have to say in my statement."

The magistrate said that did not contain a clear plea of guilty. Gandhi thereupon replied, "I do not wish to waste the time of the court and I plead guilty."

The magistrate said, "If you leave the district now and promise not to return, the case against you would be withdrawn." Gandhi emphatically said: "That cannot be. Not to speak of this time alone, I shall make Champaran my home even after my return from jail."

There was now no occasion to postpone the hearing, but as both the magistrate and the Government pleader had been taken by surprise, the magistrate postponed judgement till three o'clock.

At about one o'clock, when Gandhi was about to return to his residence, the Superintendent of Police called him. He had one time been in South Africa. He spoke against Rajkumar Shukla and promised to bring about a meeting between Gandhi and the planters. Thereafter Gandhi saw Mr. Heycock, the district magistrate, who expressed regret at the necessity he felt to launch proceedings against him and said that Gandhi ought to have seen him earlier. Gandhi replied that after the rebuff he had received from the commissioner it was neither possible nor proper for him to see the magistrate The magistrate requested Gandhi to postpone his visits to villages for three days to which he consented.

Gandhi appeared in the magistrate's courtroom at three p.m. The magistrate told him that he would pass orders on April 21 but that he would release him in the meantime on a bail of Rs. 100. Gandhi said that he had no bailor and could not offer bail. Then the magistrate said, "If you cannot offer bail, then you may offer personal recognizance." When Gandhi declined to do even that, he said : "Very well. Come back on April 21 when I propose to give my verdict." Gandhi agreed.

Shortly after three o'clock Gandhi returned to his residence and he wrote to his friends and newspapers about that day's happenings with a request not to create any agitation until the Government's orders were known.

On April 18 Mazharul Haq, Brajkishore Babu, Rajendra Babu, Babu Anugrahanarayan, Shambhusaran and Polak reached Motihari. After a prolonged discussion they decided to follow Gandhi in jail, if necessary. Gandhi immediately took down names and divided them into batches of two to carry on the inquiry and court imprisonment one after another. Mazharul Haq and Brajkishore Prasad would be in charge, if Gandhi was removed. The next batch would consist of Babu Dharnidhar and Ramnavmi Prasad. If they too were picked up, Rajendra Prasad, Babu Shambhusaran and Anugrahanarayan would continue the work. Whatever happened the ryots were not to be let down. In accordance with this decision Haq and Brajkishore Prasad left for Patna and Darbhanga respectively to settle their private affairs, so that they might return by April 21. Mazharul Haq, who was then a member of the Viceroy's Legislative Council, sent a telegram to the Viceroy, detailing the happenings in Champaran.

From April 19 batches of tenants began to pour in and Gandhi's assistants recorded their statements. Gandhi himself recorded statements of some of the tenants and he read the statements recorded by others. Those who were entrusted with the work were told to cross-examine the tenants carefully and closely, to record only such statements as appeared to them to be true, and if they came across any case which required immediate inquiry to draw Gandhi's attention to it.

On the 20th the statements continued to be recorded the whole day. A stream of peasants poured in from 6.30 a. m. to 6. 30 p. m. Many had to stay overnight and still their statements could not be recorded even the next day.

At about 7 p. m. the magistrate sent a written message that the Lieutenant-Governor had ordered the case against Gandhi to be withdrawn and the collector wrote saying that he was at liberty to conduct the proposed inquiry, and that he might count on whatever help he needed from the officials. When he called on the Collector Mr. Heycock that evening, he told Gandhi that he might ask for whatever papers he desired to see, and that he was at liberty to see him whenever he liked.

"The country thus had its first direct object lesson in civil disobedience," observed Gandhi. "The affair was freely discussed both locally and in the press, and my inquiry got unexpected publicity."

An intimate account of the methods of the inquiry, in Gandhi's own words, is as follows :

"The inquiry could not be conducted in Gorakh Babu's house, without practically asking him to vacate it. And the people of Motihari had not yet shed their fear to the extent of renting a house to us. However, Brajkishore Babu tactfully secured one with considerable open space about it, and we now removed there.

"It was not quite possible to carry on the work without money. It had not been the practice hitherto to appeal to the public for money for work of this kind. Brajkishore Babu and his friends were mainly vakils who either contributed funds themselves, or found it from friends whenever there was an occasion. How could they ask the people to pay when they and their kind could well afford to do so ? That seemed to be the argument. I had made up my mind not to accept anything from the Champaran ryots. It would be bound to be misrepresented. I was equally determined not to appeal to the country at large for funds to conduct this inquiry. For that was likely to give it an all-India and political aspect. Friends from Bombay offered Rs. 15,000, but I declined the offer with thanks. I decided to get as much as was possible with Brajkishore Babu's help, from well-do-do Biharis living outside Champaran and, if more was needed, to approach my friend Dr. P. J. Mehta of Rangoon. Dr. Mehta readily agreed to send me whatever might be needed. We were thus free from all anxiety on this score. We were not likely to require large funds, as we were bent on exercising the greatest economy in consonance with the poverty of Champaran. Indeed it was found in the end that we did not need any large amount. I have an impression that we expended in all not more than three thousand rupees, and, as far as I remember, we saved a few hundred rupees from what we had collected.

"The curious ways of living of my companions in the early days were a constant theme of raillery at their expense. Each of the vakils had a servant and a cook, and therefore a separate kitchen, and they often had their dinner as late as midnight. Though they paid their own expenses, their irregularity worried me, but as we had become close friends there was no possibility of a misunderstanding between us, and they received my ridicule in good part. Ultimately it was agreed that the servants should be dispensed with, that all the kitchens should be amalgamated, and that regular hours should be observed.

As all were not vegetarians, and as two kitchens would have been expensive, a common vegetarian kitchen was decided upon. It was also felt necessary to insist on simple meals.

"These arrangements considerably reduced the expenses and saved us a lot of time and energy, and both these were badly needed. Crowds of peasants came to make their statements, and they were followed by an army of companions who filled the compound and garden to overflowing. The efforts of my companions to save me from *darshan*-seekers were often of no avail, and I had to be exhibited for *darshan* at particular hours. At least five to seven volunteers were required to take down statements, and even then some people had to go away in the evening without being able to make their statements. All these statements were not essential, many of them being repetitions, but the people could not be satisfied otherwise, and I appreciated their feelings in the matter.

"Those who took down the statements had to observe certain rules. Each peasant had to be closely cross-examined, and whoever failed to satisfy the test was rejected. This entailed a lot of extra time, but most of the statements were thus rendered incontrovertible.

"An officer from the C. I. D. would always be present when these statements were recorded. We might have prevented him, but we had decided from the very beginning not only not to mind the presence of C. I. D. officers, but to treat them with courtesy and to give them all the information that it was possible to give them. This was far from doing us any harm. On the contrary the very fact that the statements were taken in the presence of the C. I. D. officers made the peasants more fearless. Whilst on the one hand the excessive fear of the C. I. D. was driven out of the peasants' minds, on the other their presence exercised a natural restraint on exaggeration. It was the business of C. I. D. friends to entrap people, and so the peasants had necessarily to be cautious.

"As I did not want to irritate the planters, but to win them over by gentleness, I made a point of writing to and meeting those of them against whom allegations of a serious nature were made. I met the Planters' Association as well, placed the ryots' grievances before them and acquainted myself with their point of view. Some of the planters hated me, some were indifferent, and a few treated me with courtesy."

Giving a pen-picture of his colleagues, Gandhi wrote thus :

"Brajkishore Babu and Rajendra Babu were a matchless pair. Their devotion made it impossible for me to take a single step without their help. Their disciples, or their companions—Shambhu Babu, Anugraha Babu, Dharni Babu, Ramnavmi Babu and other vakils—were always with us. Vindhya Babu and Janakdhari Babu also came and helped us now and then. All these were Biharis.

"Professor Kripalani could not but cast in his lot with us. Though a Sindhi he was more Bihari than a born Bihari. I have seen only a few workers capable of merging themselves in the province of their adoption. Kripalani is one of those few. He made it impossible for anyone to feel that he belonged to a different province. He was my gatekeeper-in-chief. For the time being he made it the end and aim of his life to save me from *darshan*-seekers. He warded off people, calling to his aid now his unfailing humour, now his non-violent threats. At nightfall he would take up his occupation of a teacher and regale his companions with his historical studies and observations, and quicken any timid visitor into bravery.

"Mazharul Haq had registered his name on a standing list of helpers whom I might count upon whenever necessary, and he made a point of looking in once or twice a month. The way in which he associated with us made us feel that he was one of us, though his fashionable habit gave a stranger a different impression."

The list of Gandhi's helpers, according to a C. I. D. report comprised: (1) Dhamidhar Prasad; (2) Ramnavmi Prasad; (3) C. F. Andrews ; (4) Mazharul Haq ; (5) Polak ; (6) Brajkishore Sahai ; (7) Shambhu Varma ; (8) Rajendra Prasad ; (9) Anugraha Narain Singh ; (10) Brahmachari Aribhusan, "vagabond of Gopalganj"; (11) Parasnath Tripathi, "outsider from Shahabad district" ; (12) Bindyabasini Prasad Varma ; (13) Chandradwip Narain ; (14) Mr. Kripalani, "dismissed professor of Muzaffarpur College"; (15) Raghunandan Prasad, "outsider"; (16) Parmeshwar Lal ; (17) Gorakh Prasad ; (18) Ganesh Datt Singh ; (19) Harban Sahai, "a dismissed teacher of Bettiah Raj School."

On April 21, a large number of peasants had come from long distance as they were under the impression that orders in Gandhi's case would be passed that day. When they heard that the case was withdrawn their joy knew no bound. The work of recording statements, however, went on uninterrupted.

On April 22, in the morning, a wire was received at the Sabarmati ashram from Motihari : "Proceedings withdrawn under instructions from Government and official assistance to conduct inquiry promised. Feel grateful to Government for withdrawal and assistance. Being splendidly helped by local pleaders and others. Messages of sympathy and help received from many quarters which encourage fellow-workers and self. During stay have already visited some villages and seen hundreds of ryots. Officials have shown every courtesy throughout inquiry. No public agitation necessary. Issues involved are tremendously great. Hope place final conclusion before Government and country. This may be published."

Commenting on the telegram, *Abstract of Intelligence*, marked "confidential," published regularly by Bihar and Orissa Police, reproduced the following from Bombay Police Extract :

"M. K. Gandhi's recent doings in Bihar have been given great prominence here, apparently at his own express desire. As to what actually occurred I have only press reports to go upon, but it appears to be a revival of his old 'passive resistance' game with improved methods in the publicity department. On the 22nd April in the morning a wire was received at the ashram from Gandhi from Motihari reading as follows... Of course, 'No public agitation,' can be read in two ways and will doubtless be given its perfectly innocent and harmless meaning that the public need not be agitated in their minds about the welfare of Gandhi or his mission, but it may also be taken to imply that if all had not gone smoothly 'public agitation,' in the more natural and everyday acceptation of the term, would have been considered necessary and would have been forthcoming at the word from Gandhi. A leaflet giving a Gujarati translation of this wire was printed and freely distributed in the city. Following up the wire, Gandhi supplied the local press here—and probably many other papers elsewhere—with a copy of his statement before the court on the 18th April. He evidently intended the sentiments expressed in it to gain the widest publicity. . . With the usual accompaniments of lip-loyalty and the profession of an eager (but unfulfilled) desire to submit to authority, it is a subtle method of inculcating the doctrine that disobedience of official orders is quite justified if the individual thinks he knows better or believes he is working in a patriotic cause. His wide dissemination of such ideas appears to be highly objectionable and calculated to have a very bad effect. One local effect of these events has been the complete rehabilitation of Gandhi's reputation as a patriot of the first order, which had been threatened with partial eclipse as the result of a movement which was gaining headway here to disparage him on account of his primitive manners and ways of life and mode of dress and his insistence on vernaculars to the exclusion of English in ordinary intercourse and as a vehicle of education."

INDICTMENT

THOSE living in the northern areas, almost at the foot of the Himalayas, wanted also to record their grievances but Motihari was not easily approachable on account of the distance. Gandhi, therefore, decided to camp at Bettiah, the principal town in the northern part of Champaran.

On April 22, Gandhi informed the collector that he was leaving Motihari for Bettiah by the afternoon train. At every station, on the way, the ryots came from long distances for his *darshan.* At 5 p.m. the train reached Bettiah. There was such a huge crowd waiting at the station that the train had to be stopped some way off from the platform to avoid any accident. As soon as he alighted from his third-class compartment, there was a deafening cry of *jai* and a shower of flowers. Such enthusiasm Bettiah had never witnessed before.

Through the pressing crowd Gandhi walked and took his seat in a carriage. The people unharnessed the horses and tried to pull the carriage themselves. He curbed their enthusiasm by threatening to leave the carriage, if they persisted. The people yielded and the horses were again harnessed. There was a dense crowd of 10,000 eager onlookers lining both sides of the main road and the carriage could move but slowly and with greatest difficulty, till it reached Hazarimal's dharmashala, where he camped throughout his stay in Bettiah.

On the following day Gandhi met Mr. W. H. Lewis, the subdivisional officer, and Mr. Whitty, the manager of the Bettiah Raj. The collector had already informed them about Gandhi's mission.

At Bettiah a large number of tenants visited Gandhi's camp to give their statements. The work at Motihari continued and the statements which were recorded there were sent every night to Gandhi through a messenger.

Gandhi's camp at the dharmashala hummed with activity. To cope with the work, the number of assistants had to be increased. Only urgent and serious cases were immediately brought to Gandhi, who referred them to the officials or planters for relief or explanation. He sent also his own men to inquire into the grievances on the spot and in some cases, he visited the places himself to study the situation.

The villagers clamoured for his *darshan* but he satisfied their curiosity only at fixed hours. There were no public prayer meetings those days but he took his evening walks regularly and sometimes people followed him. During the walks he discussed with his assistants the questions that had arisen during the day and also fixed up the programme for the following day. He walked briskly, barefooted and often barebodied.

The workers stayed with him in the dharmashala, day and night. All had to rise early, take their bath near a well, wash their clothes and fill up the pitchers of water for drinking purpose. They did not always have to draw water from the well, for a number of tenants were often around to give a helping hand. No one was allowed to keep a servant because Gandhi wanted his colleagues to be self-reliant. For the whole party of about twenty men there was only one cook and the food served was simple. When Kasturba Gandhi joined the camp, she was put in charge of cooking, whereas Gandhi served the food. His own meals consisted of groundnuts and dates. He took some mangoes during the season. He started eating cereals only when Kasturba took charge of the kitchen.

Apart from light breakfast, the workers took two meals every day, one at eleven o'clock in the morning and the other at five in the evening. After the evening meals most of the workers would take a long walk with Gandhi. The work of recording statements commenced by sunrise and continued till sunset. The workers took a short rest after the morning meals. The statements were recorded in English and several copies were made with the help of typists who were staying in the dharmashala and working in the Survey Settlement Department. They offered their services free and worked during their leisure hours. About 25,000 tenants gave their statements—10,000 in full and the rest briefly. Thousands of statements were typed and the copies were deposited in different places for safety.

Gandhi worked the hardest. He studied statements and carried on correspondence till late in the night and woke up early to cope with the heavy work. He slept and worked on the open terrace of the dharmashala and occupied a space, three feet by six feet, in a passage on the staircase.

On the third day of his stay in Bettiah, he visited the Laukaria village in the company of Brajkishore Prasad who recorded the cultivators' statements. Mr. Lewis who happened to be there was struck by the newly acquired boldness of the ryots and their eagerness to give detailed statements. Gandhi met Mr. Gale, the manager of the Byreah factory, and had a long discussion about the ryots' grievances with him. He spent the night in the village and returned to Bettiah on foot the next day.

On April 27 Gandhi went to see Rajkumar Shukla's house at Murali Bharahwa which had been looted by the factory servants a month earlier. To reach the village he started on foot from Narkatiaganj railway station. He walked about seven miles in the scorching heat and reached the village at about ten o'clock. He was shocked to see the devastated condition of Rajkumar's property. A large number of ryots gave statements about the loot, describing in detail the vandalism. Gandhi went and saw Mr. A. C. Amman, the manager of Belwa factory, who was a terror to cultivators. Gandhi and his colleagues spent the night with the villagers and the following morning they all returned to Bettiah.

After his return from Belwa Gandhi again went and saw Mr. Lewis and Mr. Whitty. The planters and the local officers were much upset by Gandhi's visit. Mr. Lewis was very apprehensive and had drawn before his imagination a terrible picture of a likely disturbance and had come to the conclusion that the ryots held the officials in scant respect. Mr. Lewis thought that Government must take some steps to curb Gandhi's activities. Gandhi discussed the new developments with his workers at great length. The workers thought that under the Defence of India Act they all might be externed from Champaran and that the thousands of statements they had recorded might be confiscated.

Gandhi said that the Government might deal with them as they liked but it would be an act of supreme folly on the Government's part to forfeit or destroy the evidence that they had collected. They should never do any such things, beacuse if they destroyed that evidence then any statement that workers might make would have to be accepted, and the Government would expose themselves to attack on all sides without gaining anything. But as a precautionary measure it was desirable to have more than one copy of all the papers. The discssion went on till late at night.

At about 8 p.m. Gandhi received a copy of the report prepared by Mr. Lewis for submitting to the Government. Gandhi returned the report with his note the same night. His note, dated April 28, addressed to Mr. Lewis said :

"I have your note of even date. I thank you for having sent me your letter to Mr. Heycock for perusal. I appreciate the frankness that pervades it and it is on the whole a very fair summary of what has happened between us.

"As to the guns, I think you are somewhat unnecessarily offended. I mentioned the matter to you on Mr. Heycock's suggestion, and if you admit the propriety of my having spoken to you about the matter, I could not be blamed for having told the aggrieved parties that there was a probability of their getting back their guns. This, if anything, was done to create a good impression about yourself, an impression which, I am happy to say, I carried with me when I first met you and which I have had no reason to change since. There was certainly no interference on my part with your authority.

"I venture to think that your deduction too that in the estimation of the ryots I am superseding local authority is hardly warranted by facts. My mission is to invoke the help of local authority in their aid, and to stimulate its interest in them more fully than heretofore.

"I anticipate no trouble because I always make it a point to seek an interview with the planters wherever I go, to tell the people that relief is to come not from me, but from the planters and the Government, and that they are in no case to use violence or stop work, but continue it as before as if there was no inquiry being made by me, and also because the inquiry is absolutely open and attended by the representatives of the police department as also the planters.

"You are less than fair to Babu Brajkishore Prasad. Together with other friends from Bihar he is helping me very materially. In this inquiry he has no status apart from me ; hence he and the other friends have not called on you. But I must state that their assistance has been of the greatest value to me.

"Perhaps it is but fair to the planters to say that Mr. Still has of his own motion invited me to visit his *dehat* and remain there as long as I like and that Mr. Cox has written to me saying that he is arranging a meeting with some leading planters and concludes: 'You may be sure that we wish to assist you in your inquiry.' This perhaps is in conflict with your statement 'By the planters he (I) is regarded with great suspicion as their natural enemy.'

"I want to serve my countrymen and the planters through the Government where their assistance is necessary."

At the invitation of the planters Gandhi went to Motihari to attend their meeting on May 2. There was a long discussion but nothing came out of it. On the following day he returned to Bettiah after meeting Mr. Heycock, the District Magistrate, and Mr. Sweeney, the Settlement Officer.

The Government received official reports of Gandhi's activities and also letters of complaints from the planters who expected serious trouble.

On May 5 Mr. Cox and Mr. Jameson, the representatives of the Champaran branch of Indigo Planters' Association, met the Lieutenant-Governor at Ranchi to complain about Gandhi's inquiry.

The Lieutenant-Governor explained the attitude of the Government towards the present situation in Champaran. He remarked that Gandhi had no official recognition of any sort. It was a free country, however, and the local government were not in a position to interfere with any mission of inquiry. He instanced, by way of illustration, the inquiry made by Mr. C. F. Andrews in Fiji. Government would have placed themselves in a false position by preventing the inquiry. They were, however, prepared to take action if anything prejudicial to the public safety occurred.

"The result of Gandhi's inquiry will not bind Government in any way," he said. "The appointment of a commission is both unnecessary in view of the settlement operations and objectionable in that it would involve official recognition of Gandhi."

Mr. Cox explained that they had only mentioned a commission to show that if it were considered a possible way out of the present difficulty the planters would welcome one.

Mr. Jameson said that Gandhi was not now paying much attention to the legal points in dispute between the planters and the ryots, such as *sharahbeshi*; he was giving most of his attention to questions of a more personal nature, such as labour rates, the alleged employment of children in factory work, and so on. The chief danger, however, arose not from the inquiries themselves, but from the fact that the people as a whole were being worked up through the name of Mr. Gandhi.

Asked whether it would do any good to issue a general notice that Gandhi has no official recognition or authority to settle disputes, the planters said that such a notice would never reach the people for whom it was intended, or if it did, it would be explained away.

Mr. Cox said that their interview with Gandhi had shown that he had no idea of listening fairly to the European side of the question. He instanced the case of the Belwa concern where *abwabs* had been taken with the rent from time immemorial. Gandhi's only advice to the planter was that he should rise above mercenary considerations and give up *abwabs*.

Mr. Cox stated that none of the Bettiah planters had come to Ranchi with the deputation because they were afraid to leave their factories, the people being in such an excited frame of mind.

Adverting to the dangerous nature of the present position, Messrs Cox and Jameson explained that the crops were now on the gound and the result of the present agitation would be the spread of a system of passive resistance. The ryots would pay no rent and would neither give their labour nor their carts. This would spell ruin for the planters. The general feeling amongst the local zamindars and well-disposed people was amazement that the sirkar should have allowed the present state of things to come to pass. Further inaction would confirm the local belief that Gandhi had been sent by the Viceroy to supersede the local administration. "The people say that he could not be put in jail and that his mission cannot now be stopped. They see numerous courts of inquiry being held all over the district and they are told they have only to tell their grievances to Gandhi and they need not have anything more to do with the factories. There will be no improvement in the tenseness of local feelings so long as Mr. Gandhi remains in the district, for there is constant coming and going between the leading local agitators of all portions of the district and Mr. Gandhi's followers."

The Lieutenant-Governor promised to review the whole situation but he emphasized that it would be difficult to take any action unless there was tangible evidence of the mischievous results accruing from Gandhi's campaign.

On May 6 Gandhi received a telegram from Mr. McPherson, the Chief Secretary to Government, from Ranchi, informing him that the Hon'ble Mr. W. Maude, the Revenue Member, would be going to Patna on May 10 and requesting Gandhi to meet him there.

On May 9, Gandhi accompanied by Brajkishore Prasad reached Patna to meet Mr. Maude. Almost all the leaders of Patna and a large number of admirers received him at the station, from where he went to Mazharul Haq's house. On May 10 Gandhi had an interview with Mr. Maude for about two hours. Mr. Maude told him to submit his report to the Government, who would then consider what action should be taken on it. He added that his inquiry had caused a great deal of excitement and uneasiness amongst the planters. He said that the Government had confidence in Gandhi and would not mind if he carried on the inquiry himself. But the lawyers who were working with him were old agitators, and they had joined him, not to help the ryots, but to serve their own selfish ends and to get an opportunity to shine as lawyers. He, therefore, asked Gandhi to remove them. Gandhi replied that he would send the report on his return to Bettiah and would, instead of detailed statements, have their summaries recorded to save time. As regards the removal of his co-workers, he told Mr. Maude plainly that that was not possible.

On May 11 Gandhi returned to Bettiah and began to write his short report based on the lengthy one prepared by his co-workers. The detailed report had not only listed all the complaints but also had given a brief summary of the voluminous evidence. Gandhi did not cite any evidence, but generally stated that those complaints were substantiated by proofs in his possession. Gandhi's short report read as follows :

"In accordance with the suggestion made by the Hon'ble Mr. Maude, I beg to submit herewith the preliminary conclusions which I have arrived at as a result of the inquiry being made by me into the agrarian conditions of the ryots of Champaran.

"At the outset I would like to state that it was not possible for me to give the assurance which Mr. Maude would have liked me to have given, namely, that the vakil friends who have been assisting me would be withdrawn. I must confess that this request has hurt me deeply. It has been made ever since my arrival here. I have been told, that is, after the withdrawal of the order of removal from the district, that my presence was harmless enough and that my *bona fides* were unquestioned, but that the presence of the vakil friends was likely to create a 'dangerous situation'. I venture to submit that if I may be trusted to conduct myself decorously, I may be equally trusted to choose helpers of the same type as myself. I consider it a privilege to have the association in the difficult task before me of these able, earnest and honourable men. It seems to me that for me to abandon them is to abandon my work. It must be a point of honour with me not to dispense with their help until anything unworthy is proved against them to my satisfaction. I do not share the fear that either my presence or that of any friends can create a 'dangerous situation'. The danger, if any, must be in the causes that have brought about the strained relation between the planters and the ryots. And if the causes were removed, there never need be any fear of a 'dangerous situation' arising in Champaran so far as the ryots are concerned.

"Coming to the immediate purpose of this representation I beg to state that nearly 4,000 ryots have been examined and their statements taken after careful cross examination. Several villages have been visited and many judgements of courts studied. And the inquiry is, in my opinion, capable of sustaining the following conclusions.

"Factories or concerns in the district of Champaran may be divided into two classes :

"Those that have never had indigo plantation and those that have.

"The concerns that have never grown indigo have exacted *abwabs* known by various local names equal in amount at least to the rent paid by the ryots. This exaction, although it has been held to be illegal, has not altogether stopped.

"The indigo-growing factories have grown indigo either under the *tinkathia* system or *khuski.* The former has been more prevalent and has caused the greatest hardship. The type has varied with the progress of time. Starting with indigo it has taken in its sweep all kinds of crops. It may now be defined as an obligation presumed to attach to the ryot's holding whereby the ryot has to grow a crop on 3/20 of the holding at the will of the landlord for a stated consideration. There appears to be no legal warrant for it. The ryots have always fought against it and have only yielded to force. They have not received adequate consideration for the services. When, however, owing to the introduction of synthetic indigo the price of the local product fell, the planters desired to cancel the indigo *sattas.* They, therefore, devised a means of saddling the losses upon the ryots. In lease-hold lands they made the ryots pay *tawan,* that is, damages to the extent of Rs. 100 per bigha in consideration of their waiving their right to indigo cultivation. This, the ryots claim, was done under coercion. Where the ryots could not find cash, hand-notes and mortgage deeds were made for payment in instalments bearing interest at 12 per cent per annum. In these the balance due has not been described as *tawan,* that is, damage, but it has been fictitiously treated as an advance to the ryot for some purpose of his own.

"In *mokarri* land the damages have taken the shape of *sharahbeshi sattas,* meaning enhancement of rent in lieu of indigo cultivation. The enhancement according to the survey report has in the case of 5,955 tenancies amounted to Rs. 31,062, the pre-enhancement figure being Rs. 53,865. The total number of tenancies affected is much larger. The ryots claim that these *sattas* were taken from them under coercion. It is inconceivable that the ryots would agree to an enormous perpetual increase in their rents against freedom from liability to grow indigo for a temporary period, which freedom they were strenuously fighting to secure and hourly expecting.

"Where *tawan* has not been exacted the factories have forced the ryots to grow oats, sugarcane or such other crops under the *tinkathia* system. Under the *tinkathia* system the ryot has been obliged to give his best land for the landlords' crops: in some cases the land in front of his house has been so used ; he has been obliged to give his best time and energy also to it so that very little time has been left to him for growing his own crops—his means of livelihood.

"The cart-hire *sattas* have been forcibly taken from the ryots for supplying carts to the factories on hire insufficient even to cover the usual outlay. Inadequate wages have been paid to the ryots where labour has been impressed and even boys of tender age have been made to work against their will.

"Ploughs of the ryots have been impressed and detained by the factories for days together for ploughing factory lands for a trifling consideration and at a time when they have required them for cultivating their own lands.

"*Dasturi* has been taken by the notoriously ill-paid *amlas* out of the wages received by the labourers often amounting to the fifth of their daily wages and also out of the hire paid for the carts and in some villages the Chamars have been forced to give up to the factories the hides of the dead cattle belonging to the ryots. Against the carcasses the Chamars used to supply the ryots with shoes and leather straps for ploughs, and their women had to render services to the latters' families at childbirth. Now they have ceased to render these valuable services. Some factories have opened hide godowns for the collection of such hides.

"Illegal fines, often of heavy amounts, have been imposed by the factories upon ryots who have proved unbending.

"Among the other (according to the evidence before me) methods adopted to bend the ryots to their will the planters have impounded the ryots' cattle, posted peons in their houses, withdrawn from them barbers', dhobis', carpenters' and smiths' services, have prevented the use of the village wells and pasture lands by ploughing up the pathway and the lands just in front of or behind their homesteads, have brought or promoted civil suits or actual physical force and wrongful confinements. The planters have successfully used the institutions of the country to enforce their will against the ryots and have not hesitated to supplement them by taking the law into their own hands. The result has been that the ryots have shown an abject helplessness, such as I have not witnessed in any part of India where I have travelled.

"They are members of the District Board and assessors under the Chaukidari Act and keepers of pounds. Their position as such has been felt by the ryots. The roads which the latter pay for at the rate of half an anna per rupee of rent paid by them are hardly available to them. Their carts and bullocks which perhaps most need the roads are rarely allowed to make use of them. That this is not peculiar to Champaran does not in any way mitigate the grievance. I am aware that there are concerns which form exceptions to the rule laid down but as a general charge the statements made above are capable of proof.

"I am aware too, that there are some Indian zamindars who are open to the charges made above. Relief is sought for in their cases as in those of the planters. Whilst there can be no doubt that the latter have inherited a vicious system, they with trained minds and superior position have rendered it to an exact science so that the ryots would not only have been unable to raise their heads above water but would have sunk deeper still had not the Government granted some protection. But that protection has been meagre and provokingly slow and has often come too late to be appreciated by the ryots.

"It is true that the Government await the Settlement Officer's report on some of these matters covered by this representation. It is submitted that when the ryots are groaning under the weight of oppression such as I have described above, an inquiry by the Settlement Officer is a cumbersome method. With him the grievances mentioned herein are but an item in an extensive settlement operation. Nor does his inquiry cover all the points raised above. Moreover grievances have been set forth which are not likely to be disputed. And they are so serious as to require an immediate relief.

"That *tawan* and *sharahbeshi sattas* and *abwabs* have been exacted cannot be questioned. I hope it will not be argued that the ryots can be fully protected as to these by recourse to law. It is submitted that where there is wholesale exaction, courts are not sufficient protection for the ryots and the administrative protection of the sirkar as the supreme landlord is an absolute necessity.

"The wrongs are twofold. There are wrongs which are accomplished facts and wrongs which continue. The continuing wrongs need to be stopped at once and a small inquiry may be made as to past wrongs such as damages and *abwabs* already taken and *sharahbeshi* payment already made. The ryots should be told by proclamation and notices distributed broadcast among them that they are not only not bound to pay *abwabs, tawan* and *sharahbeshi* charges but that they ought not to pay them, that the sirkar will protect them if any attempt is made to enforce payment thereof. They should further be informed that they are not bound to render any personal services to their landlords and that they are free to sell their services to whomsoever they choose and that they are not bound to grow indigo, sugarcane or any other crop unless they wish to do so and unless it is profitable to them. The Bettiah Raj leases given to the factories should not be renewed until the wrongs are redressed and should, when renewed, properly safeguard ryots' rights.

"As to *dasturi* it is clear that better paid and educated men should substitute the present holders of responsible offices and that no countenance should be given to the diminution in ryots' wages by illegal exaction of *dasturi.* I feel sure that the planters are quite capable of dealing with the evil although it is in their language 'as old as the Himalayas'.

"The ryots being secured in their freedom it would be no longer necessary to investigate the question of inadequacy or otherwise of the consideration in the indigo *sattas* and cart-hire *sattas* and the wages. The ryots by common agreement should be advised to finish indigo or other crops for the current year. But henceforth whether it is indigo or any other crop it should be only under a system of absolute free will.

"It will be observed that I have burdened the statement with as little argument as possible. But if it is the desire of the Government that I should prove any one of my conclusions I shall be pleased to tender the proofs on which they are based.

"In conclusion I would like to state that I have no desire to hurt the planters' feeling. I have received every courtesy from them. Believing as I do that ryots are labouring under a grievous wrong from which they ought to be released immediately, I have dealt as calmly as is possible for me to do so, with the system which the planters are working. I have entered upon my mission in the hope that they as Englishmen born to enjoy the fullest personal liberty and freedom will not fail to rise to their status and will not be grudging the ryots the same measure of liberty and freedom.

"I am sending copies to the Commissioner of the Tirhut Division, the Collector of Champaran, the Subdivisional Officer of Bettiah, the Manager of the Bettiah Raj, the secretaries respectively of the Bihar Planters' Association and the District Planters' Association I am circulating also among those leaders of public opinion in the country who have kept themselves in touch with the work being done by my colleagues and myself. The copies are being marked 'not for publication', as there is no desire to invite a public discussion unless it becomes absolutely necessary.

"I need hardly give the assurance that I am at the disposal of the Government whenever my presence may be required."

AT FIRST HAND

On receipt of Gandhi's report in May, the Government called for reports on the same from the Settlement Officer, the District Officers and the planters before June 30, 1917. The planters were perturbed and officials believed that their authority was undermined. Hectic efforts were being made to put Gandhi in the wrong and get him removed from Champaran.

Some of the planters tried to befool Gandhi. They invited him to visit their farms and factories in order to prove to him that the complaints were false. They also claimed that their employees and ryots would bear them out. When Gandhi did pay them a visit, they would call his attention to the improvements they had effected in the methods of agriculture. Some of their own servants, however, would report to the contrary, and even show the documents which went against the planters.

One such planter, Mr. A. K. Holttum, manager of the Dhokraha factory, told Gandhi that his ryots were quite happy and had nothing to complain of; that if Gandhi so desired, he could visit his estate and hear this from the ryots themselves. Gandhi accepted the invitation and a day was fixed for his visit. There were several complaints against the planter and Gandhi studied them carefully before visiting Sarisawa, which was about eight miles from Bettiah.

On May 16 Gandhi accompanied by Rajendra Prasad and Kripalani went to Sarisawa. On the way some ryots met Gandhi and complained that the planter had tutored a number of tenants to tell him that they were happy and the sahib was a gentleman. "Is that not true ?" Gandhi asked. "No," they said emphatically. He then said, "Tell me what you want to say in the presence of the planter, but let it be the truth."

In a small orchard about 300 tenants met Gandhi in the presence of Mr. Holttum and Mr. Lewis. Mr. Holttum said that his tenants did not labour under any difficulties and Gandhi could verify this fact from those who had assembled there. He then called out an old man and asked him to speak. Then, turning to Gandhi, the planter said that the old man was highly respected in the locality and Gandhi should listen to him attentively. No sooner had the old man started saying that they were quite happy under the sahib than there was a a loud protest from all sides : "You are an old man, and have already one foot in the grave. Why, then, are you taking this sin upon your head ?" The planter was thoroughly upset, for he had expected that only those tenants would turn up who would praise his management, and those who had any complaints would not only not attend the meeting but would not even have the courage to voice their grievances.

Gandhi requested them to hold their peace and let the old man complete his statement; he would hear them later on, when their turn came. The old man told his story, and was followed by a few more, who also spoke in the same strain.

It was time now for the others to speak. They complained that the planter had illegally enhanced their rent on the plea of having settled them on new land, even though in some cases no new land had been made available. The planter at once pointed out that they were not speaking the truth; for he had taken expert legal opinion before he had enhanced their rent. As a matter of fact, he asserted, he had settled them on the land which was under his personal cultivation—land from which he had substantial revenue and which he had made available for his tenants on their insistence and out of the kindness of his heart.

The ryots cried out in a body that they did not want those lands, that he should take them back and release them from the obligation of paying the enhanced rent. "Let the sahib cultivate what he can on his lands, we have no objection."

Mr. Holttum angrily said, "If they do not like this, I would make them grow indigo."

Gandhi smiled and said to the planter: "Just a minute ago you had said that *hunda* settlement had no connection whatsoever with indigo and by cultivating the *zerait* lands you would be able to make more profit than you were now getting. In these circumstances it is a matter both of profit and good name to you if you take back these lands and release the tenants from what they evidently consider to be a burden."

Mr. Holttum replied, "After all, I have also to live."

The tenants had become so fearless that at this very meeting one of them voiced his grievances against the magistrate. "No one seems to help the poor people," he said. "Here is the magistrate, who does not even do justice to us. All those who wear hats are alike. A few days ago, the planter had my house looted. Vegetable plants growing on the roof of my hutment were destroyed. Cattle were let loose in my fields, and my plantain trees were uprooted. You can see the marks of this mischief even now. When I preferred a complaint before this magistrate, he, instead of acting on it, threatened me with a cane."

Mr. Lewis got red in his face and shouted that the man was telling a lie. The complainant retorted that it was not he but the magistrate who was lying. In a huff the magistrate left the place and drove away in his car to Bettiah. Mr. Holttum too mounted his horse and rode off to his residence.

After Mr. Lewis and Mr. Holttum had left, Gandhi requested his assistants to take down the names of those who wished to surrender their *hunda* lands. The work continued up to sunset and then Gandhi and his party went back to Bettiah.

On May 17 Mr. Holttum's tenants from Dhokraha and Loheria factories went to Gandhi at Bettiah to surrender their *hunda* lands. Their names were taken down as also their signatures and thumb impressions. About 500 tenants surrendered their *zerait* lands in two days. In a letter to Mr. Holttum Gandhi wrote:

"I thank you for having come to Sarisawa and having sent your carriage.

"After you and Mr. Lewis had withdrawn, I sat with the people who must have numbered over 500 and talked to them. I told them that you wanted to do justice, that you were ready to take back the *zerait* land and that you considered that it was more profitable to you to get it back. I told them too that in your opinion the people had taken the *zerait* land from your predecessor not only willingly but most eagerly, that it was given to the ryots not in lieu of indigo cultivation but that it was given in order to relieve the ryots from liability to supply labour to the landlord. I further told them that you had shown me Mr. Barclay's letter to Mr. Gourlay confirming the view and finally told them whilst on this point that if they returned the *zerait* land you expected them to grow indigo again as before up to the termination of the period of their contracts, and I assured them that I would plead with you that it would be quite unfair to ask the ryots to revert to indigo growing (for reasons to be presently stated). I then invited those who wanted to abandon the *zerait* at once, although they had paid for the full agricultural year. As a result over 175 gave in their names there and then and men have been streaming in during the two days. The total has reached nearly 500 up to the time of writing. I enclose herewith a list of the names.

"In going through the *khatians,* the receipts and the amounts charged against the *zerait* land I find on 70 tenancies that on an average the ryots are paying you Rs. 24-5-3 for every bigha of *zerait* land. The largest amount charged is Rs. 91-7-3 per bigha and the smallest is Rs. 7-8-0 per bigha. Incidentally I observe that whilst 27 bighas of *kasht* land pay Rs. 59-13-6, 27 bighas of *zerait* land pay you Rs. 659-7-0. It seems that in the vast majority of cases the ryots hold less than one bigha of *zerait* land. The rate fixed varies with the extent of their *kasht* holding and not with the quality of the *zerait.* And they are paying as much as Rs. 1-8-0 per bigha of *kasht* land in addition to from six annas to twelve annas per katha of *zerait.* And the kathas of *zerait* seem to vary with the bighas of *kasht* and in no case amounting to more than three kathas per bigha. The average worked out for fifty villagers comes to one and a half katha per bigha. This in my opinion hardly bears out Mr. Barclay's contention. It rather bears out the ryots' contention that the settlement of *zerait* is another form of *tinkathia* and was designed to cover the losses suffered by the concern when the price of indigo fell. The ryots insist that pressure was effectively put upon them to take *zerait* land. Their contention seems to be borne out by the readiness with which they have come forward to surrender it. For the last ten years the ryots have been paying what according to the above view amounts to *tawan* for not growing indigo And the concern has received on that account an average of more than Rs. 100 per bigha of *tinkathia.* In the circumstances and regard being had to the fact that you believe it to be advantageous for you to receive back the *zerait* land, I hope you will not press for reversion to indigo growing.

"I notice that in some cases damages have been settled on kathas taken out of the *kasht* land of the ryots. I venture to think that, if you would see your way to accept my suggestion, take back the *zerait* and forgo the future damage whether tacked on to the *zerait* or to the *kasht* land, one of the sorest points of dispute between the concern and the ryots would be amicably settled and you will have set an example which would be advantageously followed by other planters.

"In describing the process adopted by the concern for recovering losses on indigo from the ryots, I have hitherto confined myself to your *mokarri* land. On *thicca* land you seem to have accepted the system followed elsewhere. You have taken hand-notes for the balance of *tawan* payable by the ryots bearing a heavy rate of interest. I suggest that the outstanding hand-notes may be cancelled. The ryots for the sake of peace and compromise should say nothing as to refund either on the *hunda* above referred to or the *tawan* already collected and of which the hand-notes represent the balance.

"As to the fines, I must confess that there is overwhelming evidence to show that they have been imposed on recalcitrant ryots. This complaint is universal. I told the ryots that you said that only nominal fines were imposed when the ryots came to you for adjustment of their mutual quarrels and that you refunded these to the winners. The ryots resolutely protested and said that the fines even as much as Rs. 25 at a time and more were imposed for the so-called offences against the concern.

"The ryots are equally firm in their complaint against your jamedar, Gokul Missir, and I would be pleased to place the evidence before you if you will care to go further into the matter.

"With reference to the method (I understand only recently adopted) of charging for permission to build new buildings or to rebuild, you. justified the charge on the ground that the earth on the ryots' tenement belonged to the landlord and if the ryots used it for building purposes, they must pay for it. I find, on looking up the Bengal Tenancy Act, that the law allows the ryots to build without any interference from the landlord so long as they build for the benefit of their holdings. It seems to me that the charge is not warranted by law and I hope that you will waive it in future.

"There remains then the question of cutting trees. The section of the Bengal Tenancy Act dealing with the subject clearly allows the cultivator to cut without previous notice to or permission of the landlord. But I understand that of late years the landlords have all over been receiving half of the timber cut. I do not know whether the custom has been proved; this is a large question which can await settlement.

"I await papers promised by you regarding the Kodai Pan. As to Sitaram Tewari I think Rs. 36 on eleven kathas is a clerical error and I venture to suggest that it would be graceful on your part to recognize the error and take the rent at the usual assessment rate.

"I would beg of you to carefully consider the points mentioned herein and if you can grant relief to your ryots in accordance with the suggestions made above I do not doubt that it will lead to a lasting peace between your concern and its ryots and, what is more, it will be a simple act of justice."

On the night of May 18 fire broke out in an abandoned office of the Dhokraha factory and a part of the house was burnt. The tenants rushed to Gandhi to inform him that the factory people themselves had set fire to the house and it was an excuse for oppressing them. Immediately Gandhi sent his assistant to make an enquiry on the spot and he sent a report to the authorities.

With reference to the report prepared by Gandhi's assistant on the Dhokraha fire, the Superintendent of Police complained : "The report practically accuses the factory of having deliberately burnt down the kutchery. Mr. Gandhi's letter practically accepts the report as true. The report accuses the factory *amla* of having removed certain parts of the kutchery before the fire took place. I wish here to ask what right Mr. Gandhi had to send out his representative to hold an inquiry into a case that was under my personal supervision and had also been supervised by the magistrate. He did not notify the local police or the factory manager that he was having a private inquiry made by his assistant. This inquiry, besides being an act of trespass *ex parte,* is a further instance of the manner in which Mr. Gandhi's mission is belittling and interferes with the executive... I anticipate serious disturbance in the near future if Gandhi and his staff are allowed to remain in the district."

The planters and the officials jointly wished that Gandhi should leave the district, for his presence proved a great source of strength to the oppressed tenants. Gandhi sensed it and wrote the following letter to Mr. Heycock, the District Magistrate, on May 20 :

"I have hitherto refrained from bringing to your notice statements which have continued to stream in to the effect that the ryots are being prevented from coming in to me and that those who have come in have been subjected to all kinds of pin-pricks by the *kothi amlas* and in some cases by the managers themselves. I have discounted some of the statements. I have taken down a few. But if what I have heard about the doings of the Belwa and the Dhokraha concerns is true, it is calculated to end, on one side at least, the friendly spirit in which the inquiry has hitherto been carried on. I am most anxious to continue and to increase the friendly spirit. I am straining every nerve so far as in me lies to so conduct my mission that nothing but goodwill should be left behind, when its labours are finished. I send you the statements taken regarding the Belwa and the Dhokraha concerns. If the statements are true, they do not reflect any credit upon the concerns in question. I enclose too my letter to Mr. Holttum which was written before I heard of the fire and which was despatched before I took the statements of the Dhokraha men last evening after 6.30 p.m.

"I can understand and even appreciate the feelings which are bound to fill those who are called upon to contemplate the prospect of having to forgo huge incomes which they have hitherto been in the habit, for a long time, of receiving from their ryots. One cannot, therefore, mind any legitimate effort on their part to hold on to what they have considered their right. But what is reported to have happened at the Belwa and Dhokraha *dehats* does not in my opinion fall under such a category.

"It is a known fact that the desire of the planters generally is that my friends and I should not carry on our work. I can only say that nothing but physical force from the Government or an absolute guarantee that the admitted or provable wrongs of the ryots are to stop for ever, can possibly remove us from the district. What I have seen of the conditions of the ryots is sufficient to convince me that if we withdrew at this stage, we would stand condemned before man and God and what is more important of all, we would never be able to forgive ourselves.

"But the mission is totally of peace. I cannot too often give the assurance that I bear no ill will against the planters. I have been told that that is true of myself but that my friends are fired with an anti-English feeling and that for them this is an anti-English movement. I can only say that I do not know a body of men who have less of that feeling than my friends. I was not prepared for this pleasant revelation. I was prepared for some degree of ill will. I would have held it excusable. I do not know that I have not been guilty of it myself under circumstances which have appeared to me most provoking. But if I found that any of my associates were in the conduct of this mission actuated by any ill will at all, I should dissociate myself entirely from them and insist upon their leaving the mission. At the same time the determination to secure freedom for the ryots from the yoke that is wearing them down is inflexible.

"Cannot the Government secure that freedom ? This is a natural exclamation. My answer is that they cannot, in cases like this, without such assistance as is afforded to them by my mission. The Government machinery is designedly slow. It moves, must move, along the line of least resistance. Reformers like myself who have no other axe to grind but the reform they are handling for the time being specialize and create a force which the Government must reckon with. Reformers may go wrong by being overzealous, indiscreet or indolent and ignorant. The Government may go wrong by being impatient of them or over-confident of their ability to do without them. I hope, in this case, neither catastrophe will take place and the grievances, which I have already submitted and which are mostly admitted, will be effectively redressed. Then the planters will have no cause to fear or suspect the mission of which I have the honour to be in charge and they will gladly accept the assistance of volunteers who will carry on the work of education and sanitation among the villagers and act as links between them and the ryots.

"Pray, excuse the length of this letter as also its argumentative character. I could not avoid it, if I was to place my true position before you. In bringing the two matters which have necessitated this communication, I have no desire to seek legal relief. But I ask you to use such administrative influence as you can to preserve the friendly spirit which has hitherto prevailed between the *kothis* and my friends and myself.

"I do not wish to suggest that the *kothis* in question are responsible for the fires. That is the suspicion of some of the ryots. I have talked to hundreds of them about the two fires. They say that the ryots are not responsible for them, that they have no connection with the mission. I readily accept this repudiation because we are incessantly telling the ryots that this is not a mission of violence or reprisals and that any such thing on their part can only delay relief. But if the *kothis* may not be held responsible for them, they may not seek to establish a connection between them and the mission. Fires have taken place before now and, mission or no mission, they will take place for ever.

Neither party may blame the other without the clearest possible proofs.

"There is talk too, about the lives of the planters being in danger. Surely this cannot be serious talk. Any way, the mission cannot render them less safe than they are. The character of the mission is wholly against any such activity. It is designed to seek relief by self-suffering, never by doing violence to the supposed or real wrong-doer. And this lesson has been inculcated among the ryots in season and out of season.

"Lastly, there is, I fear, ample proof of intimidation such as is described in the statements hereto attached. Intimidation can only mean more trouble all round without meaning the slightest relief to the planters in the shape of retention of the present system.

"I seek such help as you can vouchsafe in the circumstances I have ventured to place before you.

"I am sending a copy to Mr. Lewis."

In the evening of May 20 Gandhi had a discussion with Mr. Lewis, the subdivisional officer. Mr. Lewis sent his impressions of the meeting in a report dated May 21 to the district magistrate :

"I asked Mr. Gandhi yesterday what he proposed to do, if he saw the likelihood of disturbances becoming general, reminding him of his own words to me, when I first met him, that 'at the first sign of disturbance, he would turn his back on Champaran.' He corrected me saying that I should quote him as having said 'at the first sign of disturbance on the part of those on whom he relies, that is, the ryots': from which I gather and am confirmed by his *ex parte* opinion in the Sarisawa fire that if disturbances occur, Mr. Gandhi will inevitably believe all statements that the factory caused them, and disbelieve all statements that the ryots are responsible. If disturbances occur, Mr. Gandhi says that he thinks it would still be his duty to remain in the district to stand by the ryots, unless, he added, he were forcibly removed: he would then hope by personal suffering to achieve his object. . .

"Mr. Gandhi believes, as he says, that there is no Government which is not a Government of expediency, and that all Governments proceed on the line of least resistance. Moulding his plan on this theory of governmental action, his intention is to put up the ryots' case so strongly that the Government will be bound to act on it. He does not claim to be an impartial investigator : he is, as he says, the representative of an interest, and that is the ryots'. I do not think that Mr. Gandhi has any ideas of real co-operation with Government : success, to his mind, is to be obtained not by co-operation with the Government, which only ties his hands, but by pressure on it, to force it in deference to expediency to take the action he indicates. I believe this truly expresses his view, and he thinks himself strong enough to carry through his project."

Mr. Heycock strongly recommended the application of the Defence of India Act in case Gandhi did not agree to quit Champaran. In a letter dated May 23, he wrote to the Commissioner of Tirhut:

"Mr. Gandhi's inquiry is becoming more and more dangerous to the peace of the district. To show that this is so, I need only invite attention to Mr. Gandhi's letter to me. I also forward a copy of Mr. Gandhi's letter to Mr. Holttum. This letter shows how Mr. Gandhi is developing his position. His attitude is no longer one of inquiry but of interference. He is, as his letter shows, inviting the ryots to surrender the *zerait* lands and is placing certain terms before Mr. Holttum for acceptance. The planters can scarcely be expected to countenance an attitude of interference especially as they are not parties to this inquiry, did not invite it and do not want it. Mr. Gandhi is also taking up a false position. By suggesting terms he is raising the hopes of the tenants without making it clear to them that he is not in a position to secure acceptance of his terms. The result may be tension and strained feelings and possibly disturbances...

"As a remedy I would suggest adopting one of the two alternatives set forth in Gandhi's letter... There can be no possible harm in assuring Mr. Gandhi that genuine grievances will be redressed if proved. Mr. Gandhi can be given every opportunity to put forward such grievances as he is aware of. He has collected a mass of evidence and he knows or ought to know by now what the problems are. I would suggest that he be told this and asked to leave the district with his advisers until such time as Government has had time to consider the points raised and deal with them. If he agrees well and good. If he does not, he will, on the evidence of his own letters, have proved himself unreasonable and will, if the correspondence is published, forfeit all claim to any sympathy from any reasonable man if the Defence of India Act is applied as I suggest it should be applied in the event of his refusing so reasonable a proposition."

On May 24, the commissioner wrote to the Chief Secretary to Government :

"When ryots have reached the stage of bandying abuse with factory supporters regardless of a magistrate's presence, and when factory buildings are being burnt down, whether by hostile ryots or by factory *amlas* for purposes of their own, we are at a point at which there may be collisions attended by loss of life without further warning.

"As to the remedy to be applied Government may have to be prepared, should Mr. Gandhi decline to go, and decline to remove his assistants, for the arrest of himself and eight or ten others and to take measures to prevent an influx of volunteers to take their place. . .

"My own view, as the Hon'ble Mr. Maude knows, is in favour of a commission constituted, first, to verify the alleged grievances, and, secondly, to suggest practical remedies. Such a commission, if constituted so that its conclusions will carry authority, will remove the sympathies of all sensible men from Mr. Gandhi, should he decline to accept its recommendations. I place this point of view before Government, because it is the course I favour rather than that advised by Mr. Heycock, but I am quite prepared to accept whatever the decision of Government may be in the matter. I would only lay stress on the point in which we are all agreed that the situation in rapidly developing dangerous symptoms, and some remedial action is urgently needed."

The police report said that Gandhi wanted to appoint some men to remain in villages. The authorities were watching his activities with great anxiety. Mr. Lewis saw Gandhi and reported the conversation to the district magistrate :

"I questioned Mr. Gandhi on the police statement. He replied that it referred not to an immediate scheme, but to a project that was at present only foreshadowed, the intention being to distribute the volunteers through the villages, in order to teach education and sanitation to the ryots, and to afford them protection...

"Mr. Gandhi further gave me the following expression of his position. He said he realized that his presence in a village where he was expected and met by a number of people, did have the effect of causing a 'commotion', a word which he carefully distinguished from 'disturbance'. He claimed, therefore, to have proceeded with additional caution in his inquiry...

"Mr. Gandhi further claims to have made every effort to keep his mission free from all political connection. His work, Mr. Gandhi says, is to comprise the compilation of a detailed report. Every effort will, he knows, be made to secure copies of this report for publication. Mr. Gandhi only proposes to permit publication, if his endeavours to effect reforms are infructuous.

"In my last letter I may have laid too much stress on certain points of change in Mr. Gandhi's actual methods. If these, coupled with the Dhokraha incidents, were made the basis for issuing a letter on Mr. Gandhi with a view to asking him to retire, the ground might not be sufficiently sure under Government's feet. Mr. Gandhi still claims that his actions will be guided both by reasonableness and by a desire to avoid disturbance. . . I am inclined to think that if necessary he would defer local tours and remain in Bettiah and Motihari, if Government desired it. He has on occasions asked me if I wished him to do so. I have always refrained from giving him directions on this point, simply telling him that if disturbances did occur as a result of his visit to any locality, I would hold him responsible for them."

The planters were nervous about Gandhi's activities in Champaran. Mr. Wilson, the secretary of the Bihar Planters' Association, wrote to the commissioner on May 26: "In view of the numerous extraordinary rumours now current in this district concerning Mr. Gandhi and his inquiries, it would be in the public interest if the Government issued a proclamation that the investigations carried on by Mr. Gandhi and his agents are purely private and have not the sanction of the Government."

The list of rumours regarding Gandhi submitted by the Planters' Association said: "(1) That he has been sent by the Viceroy in supersession of the local authorities; (2) That he can break the indigo incidence of tenancy irrespective of civil courts; (3) That ryots under contract to work carts for planters need not carry out their obligations; (4) That he will collect from planters all the *tawan* that has been paid to them and return it to the ryots; (5) That he can obtain redress for any wrongs, in cases where petitions are put in to him now, but that he will not listen to any petitions once he has left this district; (6) That the administration of the district is going to be made over to natives like himself, and that the whole planting community is going to be abolished."

The European Association, Bihar Branch, Muzaffarpur, passed the following resolution: "(1) That the presence of Mr. Gandhi in his self-imposed mission has been accompanied by unrest and crime; (2) That his continued presence there is likely to be disastrous to the welfare of the Europeans in Champaran and the peace of the district; (3) That they request the European Central Association in Calcutta to press on the Government the absolute necessity, if they wish to maintain law and order in Champaran district, to have Mr. Gandhi and his assistants removed from there at once and also that there is great fear of lawlessness spreading to the neighbouring districts."

In a long letter to the *Pioneer,* Mr. Irwin, the manager of an indigo factory in Motihari, wrote :

"The whole movement is meretricious and Champaran has been selected for it... Champaran, with its large community of European zamindars, is eminently the place to start, with hopes of success, a class *versus* class agitation. Mr. Gandhi, I believe, is a well-intentioned philanthropist, but he is a crank and a fanatic and is too utterly obsessed with his partial success in South Africa and his belief that he has been ordained by Providence to be a righter of wrongs, to be able to realize that he is being made a cat's paw of by (1) pleaders, mukhtiars, etc. who know that planters settle free, gratis and for nothing at least 75 per cent of disputes amongst ryots which would otherwise bring grist to their mills; (2) mahajans and moneylenders whose usurious dealings with ryots have been greatly checked and who cannot now, owing to the action of the planters, acquire the debtors' best lands without the consent of the landlords and (3) by Home Rule politicians who hope to demonstrate on the, for them, happy hunting-ground of Champaran, that officials and non-officials go hand in hand to oppress the population, and so prove that the district, and incidentally all India, is misgoverned under the British Raj What do these people care for the ryot save to make use of him for their own purposes ? For the protection of the Champaran planters, one, and probably only one step is essentially necessary, and that is the removal of Mr. Gandhi from the district. The extreme forbearance of the planters has so far prevented the outbreak of any very serious disturbances, but unless Government can see its way to protecting them, they will unavoidably be forced in taking the steps necessary for their own protection."

In introducing Mr. Irwin's letter to the readers, the *Pioneer* wrote: "Mr. Gandhi has so far failed altogether to explain what particular qualification he possesses for instituting any mission of inquiry in Bihar or elsewhere in India. His escapade at Benares not so long ago suggested that he was a gentleman of extremely little discretion and one cannot help thinking it somewhat astonishing in the circumstances that the Bihar and Orissa Government should have permitted him so much licence. We now hear of him being asked by the Lieutenant-Governor to proceed to Ranchi to see His Honour about the Champaran affair. And meanwhile the good Pandit Madan Mohan Malaviya must needs consider that his presence is urgently required in Bankipore to put things straight. It is high time, we think, that the Provincial Government took measures to discourage the activities of all roving commissioners, whose interference in matters which do not concern them and with which they cannot claim to have any special competence to deal is likely to result in far more harm than good. If matters require to be investigated it is the Local Government's business to appoint its own commission of inquiry, but while the assistance of non-official Indians in the province concerned may be welcomed, there is every argument to be urged against the intervention of outsiders."

INQUIRY

On May 29 Gandhi received a summons to wait on the Lieutenant-Governor, Sir Edward Gait, at Ranchi on June 4, 1917.

The sudden call alarmed Gandhi's colleagues. The district officers had not yet submitted their comments on Gandhi's report and, therefore, the call could not be for discussing that matter. They suspected that he might not be allowed to return to Champaran from Ranchi. The planters and their supporters, the Anglo-Indian press, had been repeatedly demanding Gandhi's removal from Bihar. The local officials felt that their authority was undermined and they too had sent alarming reports to the higher authorities. "The impression that Mr. Gandhi has been sent by the king or by some other high authority to hold his inquiry has been created here and he is regarded as a new Hakim or Mulk-Malik," wrote Mr. Lewis in his confidential report. The workers wanted to prepare themselves for all eventualities and they discussed the future plan of action. Pandit Malaviya was asked by wire to proceed to Patna for consultation. Rajendra Prasad was deputed to Patna to discuss the situation with the leaders there. Gandhi called his wife and the youngest son to meet him in Ranchi.

On June 2 Gandhi accompanied by Babu Brajkishore reached Patna and discussed the situation with prominent leaders : Mazharul Haq, Pandit Malaviya, Dr. Ansari and Rajendra Prasad. It was decided that in case the Government took action against Gandhi, either Mazharul Haq or Malaviya should take charge of the work in Champaran. The same day Gandhi and Brajkishore Prasad left for Ranchi, while Malaviya returned to Allahabad.

The workers divided themselves into two groups: one was posted at Motihari and the other at Bettiah. It had been arranged that as soon as Gandhi's interview with the Lieutenent-Governor had taken place, the workers should be informed of the result by an express telegram.

On June 4 at about 10 a.m. Gandhi went for his interview with Sir Edward Gait. The interview lasted for about six hours and Gandhi reached his residence at 5 p.m., where Babu Brajkishore was anxiously waiting for the news. The workers were telegraphically informed : "Today's interview satisfactory, meeting again tomorrow."

For two days the Lieutenant-Governor discussed the situation in Champaran with Gandhi and was so deeply impressed that he came to the conclusion that the problem must be tackled at once. He, therefore, asked Gandhi to meet the members of the Executive Council and apprise them of the situation. It was ultimately decided that an inquiry committee should be appointed and Gandhi should be one of its members. Gandhi told Sir Edward Gait that he wanted to lead evidence before the commission on behalf of the tenants, and that he would not be able to do that were he to become a member. Sir Edward, however, maintained that Gandhi could, and should, place before the commission whatever evidence and information had come into his possession. He added that the complaints of the tenants had been pouring in for many years and that the Government officials had, from time to time, taken some kind of action and submitted reports. All these were treated as secret documents; still they would all be placed before the commission. None but a member of a commission could see them; if Gandhi served as a member, he would have the advantage of examining those papers and seeing for himself how far his own conclusions were supported by the Government officials. The Lieutenant-Governor persuaded Gandhi to be a member of the commission and Gandhi agreed to serve on it, on condition that he should be free to confer with his co-workers during the progress of the inquiry, that Government should recognize that, by being a member of the committee, he did not cease to be the ryots' advocate and that in case the result of the inquiry failed to give him satisfaction he would be free to guide and advise the ryots as to what line of action they should take. It was also agreed that the decisions arrived at should be treated as confidential and that the Government alone should make them public in due course. The names of other members were also settled, but as their consent had not yet been obtained, it was decided not to publish their names until such consent was obtained.

On June 7 Gandhi arrived at Patna accompanied by Brajkishore, Kasturba and Devadas. In his honour a meeting was arranged in the evening and a number of people including Pandit Malaviya attended it. He was requested to make a speech but he refused to do so. Describing the function the police report said : "He sat on the floor in front of the conveners of the meeting saying he was one of the poor public and so could not make a speech. The whole meeting seems to have been a failure and Mr. Gandhi's behaviour which is not understood at all seems to have caused a good deal of amusement."

On the morning of the 8th he was surprised to read in papers the Associated Press message about the appointment of the commission. He at once wired to the Lieutenant-Governor expressing his astonishment, for he himself had given the details of the interview to none till after the arrival of Pandit Malaviya, that is, late in the evening of the 7th. When he reached Bettiah in the afternoon, he showed the newspaper cutting to his colleagues and told them to await the official announcement. The nationalist press was jubilant; the Anglo-Indian press was very sore. The *Pioneer* of June 9 under "Facts and Fallacies about Mr. Gandhi" wrote :

"As was to have been expected the more irresponsible portion of the Anglo-Vernacular press has poured forth the vials of its wrath upon our devoted head, because we had the temerity to call in question the wisdom of permitting Mr. Gandhi and his friends to prolong their investigations in Bihar. We were quite prepared for the abuse we have received; we were not altogether astonished when certain editors of papers of whose existence we were but dimly aware thought fit to draw our attention to their extraordinary capacity for vituperation; we had, however, hoped that something in the nature of an argument would be forthcoming to justify in some slight degree the course on which Mr. Gandhi and his friends have embarked. Our expectations in this respect have not been realized, and we cannot accordingly congratulate Mr. Gandhi on his champions in the press. If he has nothing better to offer in his defence than these gentlemen have urged on his behalf one can well understand the silence he has continued to preserve. We are assured that he is a gentleman without fear and without reproach. The only impression we have of him is that he is a man who shows more discretion on some occasions than he does on others. Let us quote what we had to say sixteen months ago about a certain (Benares University) incident which Mr. Gandhi's friends would apparently fain have us forget...

"Are we to conclude that the unfortunate Mr. Gandhi has once more been the victim of a certain amount of misunderstanding ? If so the question still arises whether a person who is so apt to be misunderstood is the kind of individual to be given the licence he has been enjoying to meddle in other people's affairs. 'Mr. Gandhi,' says one of his champions, 'is an Indian, Motihari is in his country, and the ryots are his countrymen,' while as for the planters of Bihar, 'their interest in this land is limited to the money they make here. They are alien exploiters and make what they can out of the estates and the ryots.' That is a familiar line of reasoning with the more extreme sections of the Anglo-Vernacular press these days when every effort has been made by Englishmen as well as Indians to win for this country a place of honour in the councils of the Empire. It is as well that Indians, in their fervour for political reform, should not forget what they owe to 'sojourners' who have so largely helped to bring India to its present state of prosperity. It is as well too that it should be recognized that India is not the exclusive preserve of the indigenous lawyer-politician and his jackals in the press. There is scope in India for the legitimate activities of all classes of His Majesty's subjects, and if this country is to progress in the future as it has done in the past it will not be through any denial of the just claims to consideration preferred either by Indians or Englishmen. The planters of Bihar have rights no less than Mr. Gandhi or any other Indian, and it is the elementary duty of Government to see that the liberty of action of any individual is not so employed as unduly to prejudice the rights of his fellow men. As for Mr. Gandhi's native country it is Kathiawar and we have yet to learn what special qualifications he possesses for instituting inquiries into the labour conditions of Champaran. There can be no doubt at all that the investigations he has been conducting- have aroused a considerable amount of ill feeling, and for this reason if for no other, it would be better for all concerned if he and his apparently inseparable friend the Pandit from the United Provinces betook themselves at once to their respective homes. It is to be hoped that the official commission of inquiry will soon be getting to work and that it will be able to conduct its proceedings in the peace and quiet essential for a proper appreciation of the issues in dispute. Every story, it has been said, has a moral if you know where to look for it, and the moral of this seems to be that in all similar circumstances, if justice is to be done and peace and order in a province are not to be imperilled, the assistance of roving commissioners, however good-intentioned, should be studiously eschewed."

The *Statesman* of even date wrote : "It is stated that the Government of Bihar and Orissa have decided to appoint a committee to inquire into the relations between the landlords and the tenants in the province. This course has presumably been taken in consequence of the unauthorized investigations of Mr. Gandhi which appear to have caused a great deal of unhealthy excitement wherever he went and to have disturbed the amicable relations between many indigo concerns and the ryots. Mr. Gandhi has doubtless a legal right to study the land question or the indigo industry if he is so disposed, but when his researches developed into proceedings resembling those of a tribunal, and the cultivators, collected in crowds by wily agitators, came to lay their grievances before the redoubtable champion of Indian rights, his tour became an obvious source of danger. Mr. Gandhi may be credited with the best intentions. His self-denying life in South Africa and his strenuous fight for justice to his fellow countrymen are well known and have earned for him the respect of all who know his history. But in dealing with a complicated agrarian situation which has a background of heated controversy and violence it is not enough to be well-meaning. It is highly probable, moreover, that Mr. Gandhi has been used for their own ends by persons who do not possess his disinterestedness or his desire for justice. General Smuts the other day described himself as a barbarian from the veldt, and his old antagonist, Mr. Gandhi, might employ the same humorous exaggeration. Among the subtle pleaders and legal practitioners of Bihar he is a simple country cousin, and it is to be feared that he has been much imposed upon. At any rate, when arson and other exhibitions of violence followed his inquiries it was clear that the Government could not remain passive spectators. They would have been justified in bringing his tour to an end, but this step would have created a false impression, for it would have suggested that the Government wish to turn a blind eye to the grievances, real or imaginary, of the cultivators. The only way, therefore, out of the difficulty is that Government should themselves institute an inquiry. Such an investigation must necessarily be comprehensive. It cannot be limited to the particular class of grievances in which Mr. Gandhi was interested. A restriction of this kind would imply that only the relations between indigo planters and ryots were unsatisfactory and would be an unmerited reflection upon those engaged in one much-tried industry. There is no reason whatsoever for supposing that cultivators on indigo estates are oppressed while those who till the soil on ordinary zamindaris are treated with generosity and consideration. . . But, while the ryots have many and grave grievances, it does not follow that the cultivators are guileless toilers and the landlords are exacting oppressors. Both the parties have complaints to urge against the existing law, which, indeed, in some instances, militates against the praiseworthy enterprise of good landowners. A really competent and careful inquiry is needed, and ought to be of benefit to all classes of the agricultural community."

According to the assurance given to the Lieutenant-Governor Gandhi stopped the taking of statements in Bettiah from June 7 and in Motihari from June 12. On the 13th Gandhi wrote from Bettiah to Mr. McPherson, the Chief Secretary :

"I went over to Motihari yesterday and formally stopped the taking of statements. I have told the ryots that the Government are about to appoint a committee of inquiry which is likely to commence its work about the middle of July next and which will listen to their tale in so far as it may be necessary. And I have told them that in view of the above-mentioned decision of the Government, it is no longer necessary for me to take their statements.

"I am shifting the headquarters to Motihari where my work and that of my colleagues will consist in studying and analysing the evidence we have already collected and in putting it in a presentable form. The ryots will still continue to come to us for information and guidance. I do notice that to allow them to talk to us in any manner they choose is a great relief to them and they readily accept the advice that is given to them. They are being told not to disturb the existing situation pending the inquiry except where it is manifestly illegal and in no case to take the law in their own hands.

"I am not leaving for Ahmedabad till the resolution appointing the committee is published and the hot controversy going on in the press has subsided a little. If you could please drop me a wire, as to when the resolution is likely to be gazetted, I shall be obliged.

"Pray send all letters to Motihari after receipt of this. I am in Bettiah all day tomorrow (Thursday)."

The Champaran Agrarian Enquiry Committee was appointed by the Government of Bihar and Orissa in a resolution dated the 10th June 1917 which was released to the press on the 12th :

"On various occasions during the past fifty years the relations of landlords and tenants and the circumstances attending the growing of indigo in the Champaran district have been the cause of considerable anxiety. The conditions under which indigo was cultivated when the industry was flourishing required adjustment when it declined simultaneously with a general rise in the prices of food grains; and it was partly on this account and partly owing to other local causes that disturbances broke out in certain indigo concerns in 1908. Mr. Gourlay was deputed by the Government of Bengal to investigate the causes of the disturbances; and his report and recommendations were considered at a series of conferences attended by the local officers of Government and the representatives of the Bihar Planters' Association. As the result of these discussions revised conditions for the cultivation of indigo calculated to remove the grievances of the ryots, were accepted by the Bihar Planters' Association.

"In 1912 fresh agitation arose, connected not so much with the conditions under which indigo was grown as with the action of certain factories which were reducing their indigo manufacture and taking agreements from their tenants for the payment, in lieu of indigo cultivation, of a lump sum in temporarily-leased villages or of an increase of rent in villages under permanent lease. Numerous petitions on this subject were presented from time to time to the local officers and to the Government, and petitions were at the same time filed by ryots of villages in the north of the Bettiah subdivision in which indigo had never been grown, complaining of the levy of *abwab* or illegal additions to rent by their leaseholders, both Indian and European. The issues raised by all these petitions related primarily to rent and tenancy conditions; and as the revision settlement of the district was about to be undertaken, in the course of which the relations existing between landlords and tenants would come under detailed examination, it was thought advisable to await the report of the settlement officers before passing final orders on the petitions. The revision settlement was started in the cold weather of 1913. On the 7th April 1915 a resolution was moved in the local Legislative Council asking for the appointment of a mixed committee of officials and non-officials to inquire into the complaints of the ryots and to suggest remedies. It was negatived by a large majority, including twelve out of the sixteen non-official members of council present, on the ground that the appointment of such a committee at that stage was unnecessary, as the settlement officers were engaged in the collection of all the material required for the decision of the questions at issue, and an additional inquiry of the nature proposed would merely have the effect of further exacerbating the relations of the landlord and the tenant, which were already feeling the strain of the settlement operations.

"The settlement operations have now been completed in the northern portion of the district and are approaching completion in the remainder and a mass of evidence regarding agricultural conditions and the relations between landlords and tenants has been collected. A preliminary report on the complaints of the tenants in the leased villages in the north of the Bettiah subdivision in which no indigo is grown has been received and action has already been taken to prohibit the levy of illegal cesses and, in the case of the Bettiah Raj, to review the terms of the leases in which the villages concerned are held. As regards the complaints of the ryots in other parts of the district, the final report of the settlement officer has not yet been received, but recent events have again brought into prominence the whole question of the relations between landlords and tenants and in particular the taking of agreements from the ryots for compensation or for enhanced rent in return for the abandonment of indigo cultivation. In these circumstances, and in deference to representations which have been received from various quarters that the time has come when an inquiry by a joint body of officials and non-officials might materially assist the local Government in coming to a decision on the problems which have arisen, the Lieutenant-Govemor-in-Council has decided, without waiting for the final reports of the settlement operations, to refer the questions at issue to a committee of inquiry, on which all interests concerned will be represented."

The following committee was accordingly appointed with the approval of the Government of India :

President: F.G. Sly, Esq., C.S.I., Commissioner, Central Provinces.

Members: The Hon'ble Mr. L. C. Adami, I.C.S., Superintendent and Remembrancer of Legal Affairs, Bihar and Orissa; the Hon'ble Raja Harihar Prasad Narayan Singh, Member of the Bihar and Orissa Legislative Council; the Hon'ble Mr. D. J. Reid, Member of the Bihar and Orissa Legislative Council; G. Rainy, Esq., I.C.S.,

Historic Champaran

PLANTING HORSE.

CUTTING THE PLANT.

Indigo growers—contemporary sketches

Cultivators' quarters
A planter's kutchery

Instructions for workers

The programme of study shall be given though as if I was not imprisoned, that is

1\. Villages shall be visited systematically and notes of evidence of every one examined should be taken.

2\. Where the party consents to sign the notes his signature or thumb impression should be taken.

3\. Evidence should be taken even where the parties decline to sign. Reason for refusal should be noted.

4\. Evidence of pleaders who had anything to do with the cases of the ryots should be requested and it should be after the pattern suggested for Gorakh Babu.

For this evidence as many workers as would come forward should be taken. It is to be wished that many workers would come forward who would not be deterred from pursuing that enquiry even though they may receive notices of removal.

They should quietly go to gaol if they are summoned and tried for disobedience. I suggest that no defence be offered.

The ryots should be intimated definitely not to use violence whether regarding their own grievances or regarding imprisonment of those who may come to assist them. But they can be and should be told that where they know they are being unjustly treated, that is required to plant indigo when they need not, rather than go to law, they should simply refuse to plant indigo and if for so refusing they are imprisoned they should suffer imprisonment. This requires very careful explanation. Where the workers do not understand the working of this quiet resistance or do not appreciate the force of it they may drop this point of the programme.

When the workers of this first class are exhausted or not found at all, second class workers should be enlisted to collect evidence at centres where their presence is not resented. Ryots may be quietly asked to come to such centres and give evidence. All documents should be collected and classified. The work ought not to take more than six weeks. At the end of the enquiry the whole of the evidence oral or documentary should be printed for private circulation. In the first instance if no one will print it, it should be typed. All the papers and evidence should be collected at one place and sifted and marshalled under one man's directions. Babu Brij Kishore Prasad should take it up unless Mr Andrews arrives and does the marshalling.

Further action should be taken after consultation with a small all-India committee under Pandit [illegible] or Mr Shastri. There should be a demand for an impartial enquiry containing a number (equal with that of the planters representatives) of Indians representing the ryots. Our representatives must be of our choice.

Pending enquiry planters should institute no suits for damages etc., an impartial person should be present at the time of distribution of wages daily or otherwise.

Workers should be paid where necessary. If funds can not be raised locally Imperial Citizenship Association should be asked.

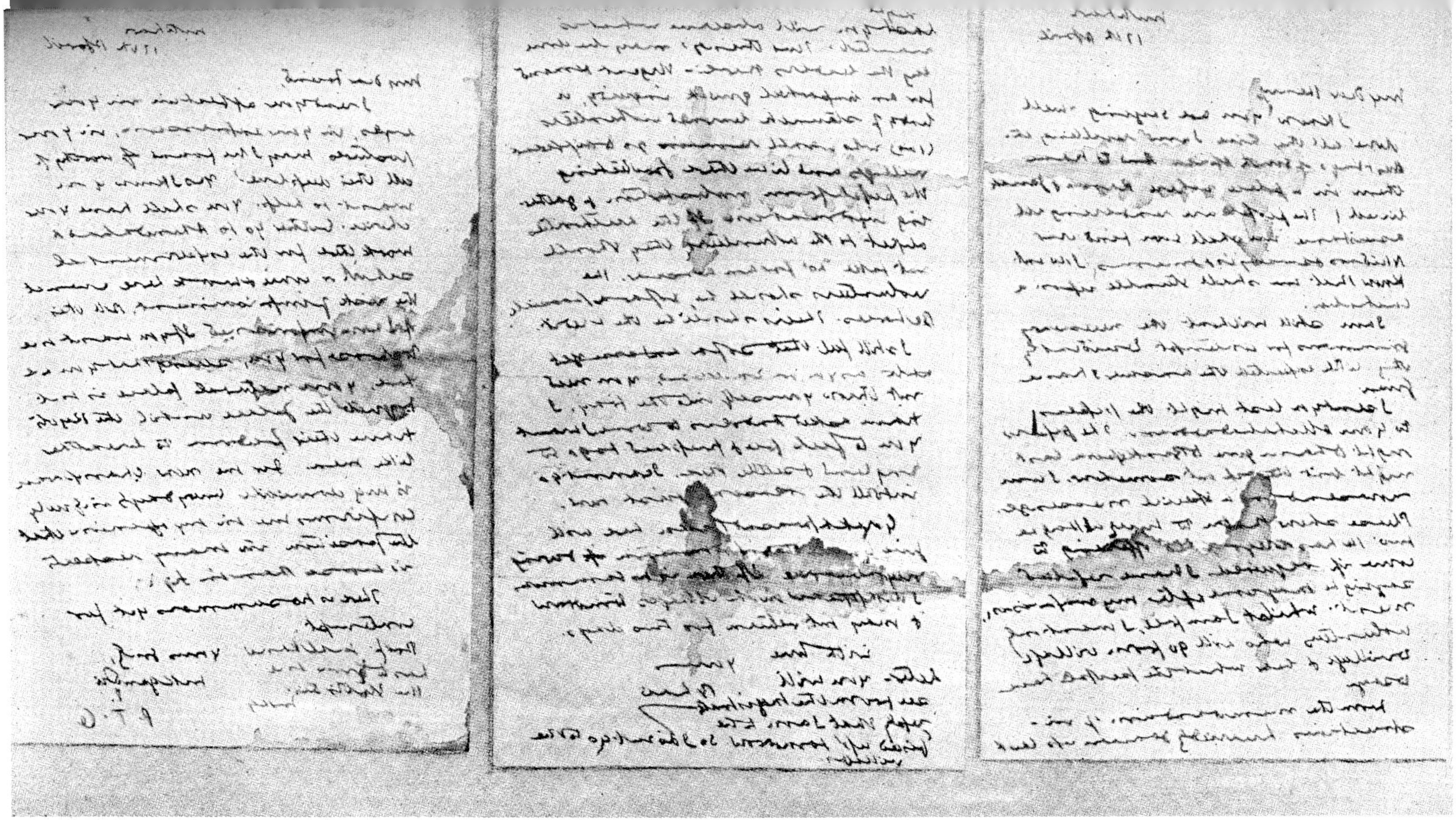

Gandhi's letters from Champaran to Mr. Polak and to a "friend"

Hazarimal's dharmashala where Gandhi camped and conducted his campaign

Confidential.

RANCHI

The 29th September 1917

D. O. No. 3423-C

My dear Morshead,

I have laid your demi-official letters of the 23rd and 24th instant regarding the Champaran situation before Government. The whole matter is under their consideration and orders will be passed as soon as the Committee's report which is expected shortly is received. It is obviously impossible for Government to take any action before that event and equally inconceivable that any local planter will be so foolish as to do anything that will prejudice the case of his fellow-planters while the Committee are still in consultation with leading members of the community.

I am to add that on the facts now before them, Government think that it would do far more harm than good to take any prohibitory action against Mr Gandhi as soon as the Committee have submitted their report.

Yours sincerely,

The Hon'ble Mr L. F. Morshead, I. C. S.,
Commissioner of the Tirhut Division,
Muzaffarpur.

A Confidential letter from the Chief Secretary, Bihar Government, to the Commissioner of Tirhut

A School at Bhitharwa built by Gandhi's colleagues on a land attached to a temple where he temporarily stayed

Deputy Secretary in the Finance Department of the Government of India; M. K. Gandhi, Esq.

Secretary: E. L. Tanner, Esq., I.C.S., Settlement Officer, South Bihar.

The terms of reference of the committee were (1) to inquire into the relations between landlords and tenants in the Champaran district, including all disputes arising out of the manufacture and cultivation of indigo; (2) to examine the evidence on those subjects already available, supplementing it by such further inquiry, local and otherwise, as they may consider desirable; and (3) to report their conclusions to Government, stating the measures they recommend in order to remove any abuse or grievances which they might find to exist.

The committee was scheduled to assemble about the 15th of July and complete its labours within three months.

Raja Harihar Prasad resigned on account of ill health before the committee assembled, and the Government appointed the Hon'ble Raja Krityanand Singh, Member of Bihar and Orissa Legislative Council.

The planters strongly protested against the appointment of Gandhi as a member of the inquiry committee and complained "that notwithstanding Mr. Gandhi's undertaking to the Government on the part of himself and his assistants to discontinue his present mission he and they are just as active as ever," and "it is hoped and prayed that the Government will take steps that he fulfils his undertaking and leaves the district immediately." An identical sentiment was expressed by the European Association of Calcutta.

The *Pioneer* wrote : "As for Mr. Gandhi's selection as a member of the committee all that need be said is that it is less open to objection than the licence previously accorded to him to conduct, to the prejudice of the planting community, an irregular inquiry of his own."

The *Statesman* wrote: "Mr. Gandhi's voluntary investigation has forced their hand. The Government do not, of course, admit in express terms that the knight-errant from South Africa upset their calculations. No one who seriously considers the matter can doubt that it would have been much better if Mr. Gandhi had not come to Bihar... But the difficulties are plain, and an Indian Government who always keep one eye on the House of Commons and the possibility of ignorant misrepresentations, may be pardoned if they decided that their most prudent course was to permit Mr. Gandhi to proceed on his tour and to risk the consequences. The inevitable results have happened, and to avert further disturbance the Government have been compelled to appoint a committee of inquiry. The selection of members has been admirably made...some special qualification can be discovered in each member of the committee, not excluding Mr. Gandhi, whose appointment is a bold and judicious stroke."

Planters engineered against Gandhi a poisonous agitation. All sorts of falsehoods appeared in the Anglo-Indian press against him and his co-workers. Mr. Irwin wrote in the *Pioneer* : "But, sir, the genuineness of Mr. Gandhi's 'mission' would have been much less in doubt if his methods had been less theatrical. Notwithstanding his familiarity in England and elsewhere with the minor amenities of western civilization, he (in Champaran at least) discards the use of head-covering or shoes, sits on the floor, cooks his own food and affects to follow the footsteps of the much greater philanthropist of 2,000 years ago; and one at least of his most devoted followers, an ex-Hon'ble Member of Council, who in his unregenerate (?) days wore English shoes and semi-Anglicized clothing, also now goes shoeless and head-coveringless and cooks his own food, etc. Firmly dealt with this agitation would have died a natural death, the sole purpose of it being to drive the non-official portion of the European community out of the district and to hand over to the tender mercies of the lawyer and mahajan the ryot for whose welfare so much meretricious solicitude is being advertised."

Gandhi wrote in reply to the *Pioneer* :

"I have hitherto successfully resisted the temptation of either answering your or Mr. Irwin's criticism of the humble work I am doing in Champaran. Nor am I going to succumb now except with regard to a matter which Mr. Irwin has thought fit to dwell upon and about which he has not even taken the trouble of being correctly informed. I refer to his remarks on my manner of dressing.

"My 'familiarity with the minor amenities of western civilization' has taught me to respect my national costume, and it may interest Mr. Irwin to know that the dress I wear in Champaran is the dress I have always worn in India, except that for a very short period in India I fell an easy prey in common with the rest of my countrymen to the wearing of semi-European dress in the courts and elsewhere outside Kathiawar. I appeared before the Kathiawar courts now twenty-one years ago in precisely the dress I wear in Champaran.

"One change I have made and it is that having taken to the occupation of weaving and agriculture and having taken the vow of swadeshi my clothing is now entirely hand-woven and hand-sewn and made by me or my fellow-workers. Mr. Irwin's letter suggests that I appear before the ryots in a dress I have temporarily and specially adopted in Champaran to produce an effect. The fact is that I wear the national dress because it is the most natural and the most becoming for an Indian. I believe that our copying of the European dress is a sign of our degradation, humiliation and our weakness, and that we are committing a national sin in discarding a dress which is best suited to the Indian climate and which for its simplicity, art, and cheapness, is not to be beaten on the face of the earth and which answers hygienic requirements. Had it not been for a false pride and equally false notions of prestige, Englishmen here would long ago have adopted the Indian costume. I may mention incidentally that I do not go about Champaran bare-headed. I do avoid shoes for sacred reasons, but I find too that it is more natural and healthier to avoid them whenever possible.

"I am sorry to inform Mr. Irwin and your readers that my esteemed friend Babu Brajkishore Prasad, The ex-Hon'ble Member of Council', still remains unregenerate and retains the provincial cap and never walks barefoot and 'kicks up' a terrible noise even in the house we are living in by wearing wooden sandals. He has still not the courage, in spite of most admirable contact with me, to discard his semi-Anglicized dress and whenever he goes to see officials puts his legs into the bifurcated garment and on his own admission tortures himself by cramping his feet in elastic shoes. I cannot induce him to believe that his clients won't desert him and the courts won't punish him if he wore his more becoming and less expensive dhoti. I invite you and Mr. Irwin not to believe the stories that the latter hears about me and my friends, but to join me in the crusade against educated Indians abandoning their manners, habits and customs which are not proved to be bad or harmful. Finally I venture to warn you and Mr. Irwin that you and he will ill-serve the cause both of you consider is in danger by reason of my presence in Champaran if you continue, as you have done, to base your strictures on unproved facts. I ask you to accept my assurance that I should deem myself unworthy of the friendship and confidence of hundreds of my English friends and associates—not all of them fellow cranks—if in similar circumstances I acted towards them differently from my own countrymen."

Regarding the planters' accusation that Gandhi still recorded the ryots' statements, the commissioner wrote to the Chief Secretary: "Statements have not been recorded by Mr. Gandhi or his assistants. Mr. Gandhi's assistants have been mainly occupied in preparing a synopsis of the evidence previously recorded. Ryots constantly come to see Mr. Gandhi and his assistants—the line taken is to counsel patience and tell them to await the arrival of the committee. They are also being told to stick to their statements and are being impressed with the necessity of doing so. Probably they are keeping in touch with the ryots by personal interviews and village agents who come to see them. Although they do not go out into the mofussil, there is nothing to prevent people coming from the mofussil to see them. It must be remembered too that a great many people merely come for what is called 'darshan', that is, to see Mr. Gandhi."

THE REPORT

On June 16 Gandhi proceeded to Ahmedabad to spend a few days at his ashram, and his assistants moved from Bettiah to Motihari to prepare the synopsis of the massive evidence so far collected. The statements of more than 8,000 tenants from about 850 villages against 60 factories had been recorded under the supervision of Gandhi. His assistants had also collected a large number of documents many of which were judgements of courts.

Gandhi accompanied by Dr. Deva of the Servants of India Society returned to Motihari on June 28 and spent a few days in studying the evidence. On July 7 he reached Ranchi to attend a preliminary meeting of the committee on the 11th to decide the procedure and extent of its inquiry. It was decided that the committee should sit at Bettiah from July 17. The members were lodged at the luxurious guest-house of the Bettiah Raj; Gandhi and his party stayed in the dharmashala—their old camp.

On July 15 a large number of tenants visited Bettiah for Gandhi's *darshan.* There were no less than ten thousand tenants on the 16th. Gandhi was busy studying the committee papers on the terrace of the dharmashala but he interrupted his work in order to meet the eager tenants. In a short speech, he explained to them that the committee had been appointed to redress their grievances, that they should not go in large numbers to the meeting place of the committee, and if they had any complaint to make they should do so before his assistants.

Written statements were received from the Bihar Planters' Association and two managers, one of an indigo and the other of a non-indigo concern, from twenty-five ryots, from Mr. Whitty, Manager of the Bettiah Estate, and from Mr. Sweeney, Settlement Officer, Mr. Lewis, Subdivisional Officer of Bettiah, Mr. Morshead, Commissioner of Tirhut, and Mr. Johnston, formerly Subdivisional Officer of Bettiah. The Bihar Landholders' Association was specially invited to submit a memorandum of its views, but replied that it was not in possession of the materials and the facts concerning the agrarian conditions in Champaran and it was not, therefore, in a position to submit a written opinion.

On July 17 the examination of witnesses commenced at Bettiah. The committee used to meet at 11 a.m. in the hostel of the Bettiah Raj school. On behalf of the planters Mr. Pringle Kennedy, a well-known lawyer of Muzaffarpur, was watching the proceedings. The tenants and Gandhi's assistants were admitted to the committee on tickets. The correspondents of leading papers were there to report the proceedings. The ryots used to come in such large numbers that they lent Bettiah a rustic look.

Mr. Sweeney was the first witness and his examination took the whole day. On July 18 Mr. Lewis was examined in the morning and Mr. Whitty in the afternoon. On the 19th Rajkumar Shukla and Sant Raut were examined on behalf of the tenants. The committee did not meet on July 20; on the following day Mr. Ross, the proprietor of Malahia factory, and Mr. Gale, the manager of Bairia factory, gave their evidence. On the 23rd Mr. Still, manager of Sathi factory, and Mr. Amman, manager of Belwa concern, appeared before the committee.

The sixth sitting of the committee took place at Motihari and as in Bettiah a large number of tenants visited the town. On July 25 Mr. Heycock, the Collector of Champaran, Mr. Jameson, the representative of the Planters' Association, and Mr. Hudson, the manager of Rajpore factory, were examined. On the 26th Mr. Irwin, the manager of Motihari factory, was examined and the committee returned to Bettiah.

On July 28 and the following day the members of the committee visited and held local inquiry at the Parsa and Kuria factories and their villages. No information was given to the tenants about the visit of the committee to their villages so that the "agitator" might not get an opportunity, as alleged by the planters, of tutoring the villagers. But in whichever direction the motor-cars carrying the committee members turned, the villagers assembled in large numbers and boldly replied to questions. The factory managers were informed beforehand so that they might keep their papers in readiness for inspection.

The committee met at Bettiah on July 30 and examined Mr. Granville, manager of Madhubani factory, and Mr. Brouche, its proprietor. Some members of the committee visited the villages of Malahia factory and examined its papers. The following day the villages of Dhokraha factory were visited.

On August 2 the committee examined Mr. Hudson, manager of Rajpore factory. About five to six thousand villagers had assembled to greet the committee members. Similarly, three to four thousand tenants were present when the committee examined the managers of the Peepra and Turkaulia factories on the 3rd and 4th of August. On the 6th Rajghat Hardia factory was visited.

On August 14 Mr. Jameson was again examined as the manager of the Jalaha factory. No more evidence was recorded after this. Gandhi, however, placed before the committee the statements of a number of tenants and a great many judgements of courts.

In all, eight public sittings were held at Bettiah and Motihari at which nineteen witnesses were examined, consisting of four Government officers, three representatives of the ryots, the representative of the Bihar Planters' Association, and twelve managers of indigo concerns. The committee members also made local investigations at eight concerns, where they examined in detail the managers together with the factory registers and accounts and the ryots who had submitted written memoranda, and then made numerous inquiries from the large bodies of ryots assembled to meet them. The voluminous official records also were studied. On the days when the committee did not examine witnesses or visit villages there used to be sessions for considering the evidence already recorded. The committee worked for six weeks.

The work of the committee for the time being came to a close in August; the next sitting was fixed to be held at Ranchi in September. On August 16 Gandhi left for Ahmedabad, leaving Rajendra Prasad, Ramnavmi Prasad and Rajkumar Shukla in Champaran.

The activities of Gandhi's assistants were closely watched by the police. "There have been no further discussions or negotiations with Mr. Gandhi regarding the continuance of his mission work in Champaran and Government would like to be kept well informed of the doings of the mission camps which he is said to have left at Bettiah and Motihari," wrote the Chief Secretary to the Commissioner of Tirhut on September 5.

Mr. Lewis, the Subdivisional Officer, reported :

"To ensure Government action Mr. Gandhi had first to create a situation in Champaran which would thrust itself on the notice of the Government and make action imperative. This plan of action succeeded and the committee was appointed. Those who agree with Mr. Gandhi that the situation required reform and that it was necessary that inquiries should be public and that the Government would not take up the questions unless publicly forced would excuse the imperfections of the method so long as Mr. Gandhi's main object to which paramount importance was attached was kept in view. From the more prejudicial position of a local officer I feel in face of the difficulties that have been created that I cannot too strongly condemn the lines on which the mission was conducted among an ignorant and credulous people.

"Since the agitation does not concern itself with local Indian zamindars, whatever their demands for labour or *abwab,* it assumes at once a definitely anti-European character. Reports have been brought to my notice of the type of rumour that is abroad. There must by now be a very large number of ryots who think that the factories are all to be closed down and the Europeans forced to leave. There were also rumours of the fines imposed on local European officials by the committee, owing to their misconduct in not listening to the ryots. A rumour is not negligible because ridiculous. There is no story so ridiculous that the ryots of the district will not believe it. I frequently brought to Mr. Gandhi's notice that all these rumours were circulated as his utterances in his name, but he could do no more than to disclaim them. As regards Mr. Gandhi's presence in the district, it cuts both ways: so long he is here his name can be used as a peg for every fresh rumour, while he uses his personal influence, which is great, in the direction of moderation...

"Signs of boycotting have been apparent ever since the mission came to Bettiah: labourers have been forbidden to work in the factory. The difficult situation which I have tried to describe is not entirely general, not equally pronounced throughout the indigo districts or European zamindaris, but it is sufficiently general to be dangerous.

"It is not at present actually anti-Government, but Government is traduced the same way as Mr. Gandhi's name is traduced. The ryots are told that they should take every step to fight and boycott the factories, as Government is with them. At the same time, the influence of the local officer over the ryot is, I regret to say, zero; and any punishment inflicted by a court on a ryot for an offence is attributed to corrupt motives. It is the inevitable result of Mr. Gandhi's inquiry which practically supplanted the official...

"With reference to the suggestion that the committee should make the closing of Mr. Gandhi's mission a condition of their recommendations I take the view that Mr. Gandhi and all his mission are mere pawns in the game. Were Mr. Gandhi to say that he would sever his connection with Champaran on the day the recommendations issue, I would not see in that a guarantee of settled conditions. In the first place the local leaders among the ryots are now a force to be reckoned with. They have eaten of the fruit of the tree of knowledge and know their strength. In 1909 they went about in mobs, broke the peace, were run in, convicted. They know now that boycott is a much more potent and less dangerous weapon. Secondly, no promise by Mr. Gandhi would bind political India; there have been several hints in the papers that Indian politicians have no intention of following Mr. Gandhi blindly: and an article which appeared in the *Amrita Bazar Patrika* to the effect that no great hopes were entertained of the committee's findings has a sinister significance.

"I rather doubt, therefore, whether much would be gained by closing the door to Mr. Gandhi, nor do I think he would ever agree to it. Members of the committee even while disagreeing with Mr. Gandhi have expressed their belief in his honesty and sincerity. He has so often claimed that he is no enemy of the planter and is anxious to secure peaceable relations. Government has now given proof of its *bona fides* in ventilating all points of grievances. Would it not be preferable to inform Mr. Gandhi frankly of what local officers believe to be the development of the situation and leave it to Mr. Gandhi to prove that he is as good as his word and is not working for the destruction of the factories, but for a settlement of points of difference ? I think it would be a mistake to drive Mr. Gandhi into opposition...

"If after issue of the Government orders, the local leaders who can point to no grievance and merely as anti-European agents continue to make the situation intolerable, I can only recommend the passing of special powers by legislation to deal with them and confine their activities... Once the ventilation of all grievances is secured, there is no reason why strong and effective measures, whether criticized or not, should not be taken and maintained against men who simply create mischief."

Mr. Whitty, the Manager of Bettiah Raj, gave his views "on the situation created by Gandhi at present and in the future" :

"Conditions are thoroughly unsettled. It is generally believed that Mr. Gandhi has come with authority which overrides the ordinary civil authority... The ryot believes that the non-official European will be cleared out and he is waiting to see how he can best secure his own interests. It is necessary to reassure him that big changes are not coming and to do something to give back the non-official European the prestige which was the chief asset in his work... Champaran is now in the condition in which agitators may easily start a dangerous disturbance.

"Taking this view I advocate absolutely definite pronouncements by Government on any question in which the committee advises reform, and at the same time a refusal, enforced by the strictest measures, to allow a continuance of agitation. The civil authorities must themselves introduce the changes recommended. Mr. Gandhi must be asked to accept the situation and to advise his followers to accept it, and leave the district.

"If Mr. Gandhi and his helpers remain and continue their mission after the recommendations of the committee have been given effect to, there will be continued trouble which may grow serious at any time and which will in any case seriously affect the position of the administration and the Europeans in India.

"There is an important European community with large financial interests in these parts. This community is in danger of being broken by unjustifiable agitation. Government must give it support as far as it can."

The Superintendent of Police, Mr. Marsham, in his confidential report said :

"There is no doubt that relations between planter and ryots have got worse since Mr. Gandhi's arrival and very much worse during the last six weeks. This state is in my opinion distinctly due to orders from Mr. Gandhi regarding the rates of labour. Rates of labour have no doubt been deliberately misrepresented to Mr. Gandhi by local agitators such as Rajkumar Shukla simply with a view to boycott factories. This labour question has now become most serious, and has already resulted in several riots and will result in many more. It is a recognized fact throughout this part of India that the malik or thikadar has the first call on all labour in his own village. Planters are not likely to sit still and forgo this first call on their labour. 'Complaints' are being brought to Gandhi's representatives that factories are compelling coolies to work for them, the complainants are told by these representatives not to work and to beat the factory *amlas* with the result that there have been cases of rioting already. . .

"There is not the slightest doubt that the ryots were told that they had every right to drive their carts on the upper roads and that they suddenly began doing so and assumed a very truculent demeanour if anybody tried to turn them off. I myself nearly had a row with two carters one day who stopped my car and were most insolent and defiant. However, as many carters have been prosecuted, carters have to a great extent thought better of it and given up using the upper roads.

"Mr. Gandhi also admitted to me that he had told ryots that they should not pay *sharahbeshi* as it was illegal. As this matter is *sub judice* before the High Court, he had no right to give any such order. I have on one or two occasions informed Mr. Gandhi that the wildest 'orders' were being circulated in the *dehat,* and also the wildest rumours; he denied having put them in circulation and denied that his helpers would do so without his orders. I do not think he has taken any particular steps to counteract the many orders attributed to him, nor does he appear to discourage ryots concerned in criminal cases from coming to him to 'complain' instead of going to the courts. On the contrary I am of opinion that villagers are encouraged to come in to see him or his assistants whenever they have a grievance against the factory. I am informed that he has given out that he or his representative will remain for a long time in the district to protect the ryots from the factories.

"As regards the actual friction and ill feeling, Gandhi's presence in the district must tend to increase this as he evidently wishes to paralyse labour and to undermine the authority of planters. He has on occasions offered to help planters to get labour if they will agree to pay his rates. Needless to say such a galling offer is refused by planters. His presence in the district is also most derogatory to the official administration, people openly saying he is above the collector and police and taking their cases to him first...

"The most serious result of Gandhi's mission is the present spirit of lawlessness throughout the district; the villagers are told by the agitators that if they are united they can do what they like, meaning that they can commit assault, riot, arson etc. if only no witnesses are forthcoming. Also villagers are told not to be afraid to go to prison, that Gandhi has been in prison twenty-one times. Such doctrine is highly dangerous and is a direct incitement to lawlessness. I am in daily expectation of hearing that some planter has been brutally assaulted, as Bloomfield was. Planters themselves realize this danger. Planters have shown the most extraordinary patience and forbearance, but there is a limit and I think many have just about reached the limit and will shortly assert their rights again.

"There is a very strong rumour all over the district that all Englishmen will be cleared out in a few months, that the Germans will win the war. I attribute many of these rumours to Gandhi's followers. If Gandhi was to entirely leave Champaran, but allowed these followers to carry on his mission, I think things would be far worse. The last month proves that. I do not mean to say the unrest would be any worse, I mean to say that acts of lawlessness are now likely to occur rather in his absence than if he were here.

"The mission has admittedly done a certain amount of permanent good, and has shown up certain irregularities which can never occur again. It should now be closed down. The mission, intended to be purely local and agrarian, has become entirely political and openly anti-European and is now developing into a Home Rule movement."

Mr. Morshead, Commissioner of Tirhut, along with the opinions of Lewis, Whitty and Marsham, sent his confidential note "on situation in Champaran, September 1917", to Mr. McPherson, the Chief Secretary. His own inquiries were directed mainly upon the leading feature of boycott. He reported that all the indigo concerns were finding it increasingly difficult to get any work done by the ryots.

Referring to Mr. Gale of Bairia factory, the commissioner wrote: "His ryots openly refuse to do indigo. His ploughmen are demanding Rs. 7-8-0 a month instead of Rs. 4-0-0. There is no lack of labour but he is only getting about 30 a day now against 200 last year. He is willing to pay any fair rates, but friendly ryots are threatened, and his men are told by others that they mean to get factories closed."

About the difficulties of Mr. Lees of Lal Saraya concern, he wrote: "Mr. Lees asked for 300 bighas for indigo on *khushki* terms last year, and got 600 bighas. His ryots were applying for advances in April, but now they put off the question. He got more carts than he wanted for first *mahai,* but at second *mahai,* the factory had difficulty in getting carts. Some witnesses who gave evidence for him in a case in the Settlement Court have had their dhobi and hajam stopped, and at present the factory can get nothing done. It is not a question of rates, as Mr. Lees already pays higher rates than elsewhere. The word in everyone's mouth is 'we are ready to go to jail.' It is difficult to realize the rents too. Mr. Lees has to file 500 rent suits, against a negligible quantity before."

"A boycott has set in," wrote the commissioner, "which naturally varies in degree and extent, and the effect of which will be more fully seen when sowings begin in a month or two months' time. But it is already in evidence, and only partly explained by grievances, and goes beyond passive resistance, because it is enforced by the intimidation of ryots who will not go with the rest."

The intention, he said, was to cause concerns to close down as they had to close down in Bengal many years ago. "It is on indigo cultivation that the exactions of *amlas* have been felt, and it may be that ryots wish to see an end of it under any system. Some of the planters believe that labour will never resist good rates for long, and Indian employers are said to be already getting anxious at the rates offered, which they expect will be demanded from them also."

The commissioner further wrote: "Mr. Gandhi has or claims to have the disinterested motive, the Patna people have the political motive, and the local men have the personal motive, which is perhaps the most stable of the three. It appears to me that Mr. Gandhi with the best non-conformist intentions has let loose forces which he cannot control, or does not wish to control. These forces are local personal interests reinforced by the notion that the sahib's time is past. This notion is easy to spread in the circumstances of the war, and readily accepted by the ignorant ryots. It is strengthened by Mr. Gandhi's personal success. The right course seems to me to be to require Gandhi to go, if he cannot be persuaded, and to leave to Government the task of removing proved grievances, moderating excesses and restoring good relations."

The commissioner concluded :

"I think it would be a fatal mistake to make too much of the difficulties experienced by factories, because that would only stimulate agitation. And for that reason I would ask this report and enclosures be kept entirely secret by Government. But there is, I think, enough without making too free an admission of these difficulties, to impress upon Mr. Gandhi that his mission had had deleterious results in setting class against class, that Government cannot allow these to continue, that whilst resolved on redressing all grievances, it will not suffer the concerns and the property they represent to be damaged by unjustifiable methods. If Government is in a position to make a pronouncement of such a policy I think a good deal of misunderstanding would be cleared away.

"If however Mr. Gandhi is resolved to pursue his mission, and his attitude is not such as to encourage the idea that he can be effectively unfluenced, then there is not much to be gained by approaching him, and it would seem better to let matters take their course. In that event we can only combat illegitimate developments, as far as they can be combated, by legitimate means, and give as much consideration as can be given to concerns that cannot immediately meet their obligations. It would, I think, have a very deleterious effect if even one concern was forced to close down. Moreover, the planters deserve consideration for the forbearance they are reported to be displaying in circumstances of difficulty and irritation. A consideration that appeals to me also is that, whatever their faults and these must be corrected, it is only to us that as our own people they can look for protection.

"I think, therefore, that they should be encouraged to hold on as long as they can should the boycott develop, and to continue to exercise forbearance, but should be assured of all such support as Government can give them against unjustifiable methods. Some of them are talking a little wildly at present of taking the law into their own hands, and if some assurance is not given, trouble may easily ensue, as conditions of provocation increase.

"The position may be summed up by saying that although the boycott has not proceeded far at present there are unjustifiable elements of trouble. But I should, however, prefer to have my own judgement confined, and I think the circumstances are such that it is desirable that a member of Government should visit Champaran unobtrusively, as soon as possible, in order to see for himself how matters stand."

In reply to the commissioner's note, the Chief Secretary wrote on September 27 :

"The whole matter is under Government's consideration and orders will be passed as soon as the committee's report which is expected shortly is received. It is obviously impossible for Government to take any action before that event and equally inconceivable that any local planter will be so foolish as to do anything that will prejudice the case of his fellow planters while the committee are still in consultation with leading members of the community.

"I am to add that on the facts now before them, Government think that it would do far more harm than good to take any prohibitory action against Mr. Gandhi as soon as the committee have submitted their report."

Gandhi returned to Bihar after five weeks' absence, reaching Ranchi on September 22. Sir Edward Gait, the Lieutenant-Governor, told Gandhi that if the committee submitted a unanimous report, it would be easy for the Government to act upon it. Gandhi was, therefore, anxious to have, as far as possible, unanimity among the committee members. This was a difficult task: Would the planters admit as valid the complaints which had been made against them ? If not, would Gandhi, who knew that those complaints were well founded, agree to drop them ? The principal grievances which called for redress arose out of the system of *tinkathia, sharahbeshi* and *abwab.* Now that indigo cultivation had once again become a profitable business because of the war with Germany, would the planters give it up ? Would they surrender the annual income of lakhs of rupees which they had managed to secure by way of enhancement of rent payable by the ryots ? And would they agree to refund the large amounts they had exacted from them ? All these appeared to be impossible of realization; but if that could not be achieved, the purpose of the committee would be defeated. To get over the formidable obstacles, Gandhi, at the very outset, told the committee that if the other members agreed with him, he would not insist that it should go into and express its opinion on the acts of oppression alleged against the planters, for if it did go into the allegations of the ryots, it could not but accept them as true. If, however, the members differed on this point and if Gandhi felt bound to write a separate note on the oppression by planters, he could put up a report supported by such a large body of irrefutable evidence that it could not be challenged by anybody. If the other members took a contrary view in favour of the planters, every point they would make would be contradicted by the reports of Government officials. Gandhi's suggestion was, therefore, accepted by the other members as well as the representatives of planters, for it saved them from an awkward position. Gandhi gave this advice because he felt that the excesses so far committed and the sufferings so long borne by the tenants could not be undone at this stage, and if their refutation could be effectively provided against, it was no use raking up the past.

The committee met several times and the managers of the three largest concerns—Motihari, Turkaulia and Peepra—were summoned to Ranchi for discussion on *sharahbeshi* on September 29. According to Mr. Irwin, manager of Motihari concern, an agreement was reached thus :

"We were begged to reconcile Mr. Gandhi by increasing our concession. I said our former offer having been rejected and withdrawn the present discussion was on new lines. Mr. Sly said, 'certainly not; the position is just as we left it at Bettiah,' and the withdrawal of our offer would place us in an utterly false position as neither the Government nor anyone else would believe that we had done anything but resile from our own offer. Unfortunately we could not gainsay this. Knowing our Government as we do, we quite understood that every advantage would be taken of us, so we consented to let the offer stand. After endless discussion Mr. Gandhi again refused to accept 25 per cent, but he said that he would accept any advance on that offer. Mr. Norman of Peepra tentatively asked him if he would accept 26 per cent, and to our surprise, and I must admit my deep chagrin, he accepted. There was nothing for it now to agree—having acknowledged our continued liability for 25 per cent, it would have been merely hair-splitting to hold out against one per cent more. To show you how liberal it was: It means to Motihari Ltd. alone a remission of rent amounting to Rs. 13,000 yearly, the capitalized value of which is Rs. 2,60,000 to be given to ryots who not only have never asked for it, but who have paid it for several years past without a rent suit ever having had to be instituted for a single item of it, and who all filed petitions in the current survey revision operations to say their rents were fair and equitable and mutually agreed upon , and as such they were passed by the Settlement Officer."

On the abolition of the *tinkathia* system Gandhi was adamant and the Government readily agreed. The planters did not resist him because they realized that the *tinkathia* was most hated by the ryots. According to Gandhi, whatever the terms and conditions under which the *tinkathia* system was abolished, it would be impossible for the planters to continue long after its abolition because the system was grounded on oppression; and if that oppression ceased, the planters could not stay. The effect of the abolition of *tinkathia* and the fearlessness which had been engendered in the hearts of the tenants could not but lead them to resist any oppression by the planters.

After prolonged discussions the members of the inquiry committee signed a report on October 3, 1917 which was in favour of the ryots. The report and the evidence were published in two volumes, consisting of 24 pages and 164 pages respectively, under the title "Report of the Committee on the Agrarian Conditions in Champaran". It contained the conclusions arrived at by the committee, and a number of recommendations which, with a single exception, were unanimous.

From Ranchi Gandhi returned to Champaran. On October 11th when he left Motihari for Bettiah, some 400 people were there at the station to see him off. Reporting his welcome at the Bettiah railway station the C.I.D. note said :

"About 4,000 people were present. No sooner the train stopped than people began to shout "Gandhiji ki jai', 'Gandhi Maharaj ki jai'. There were *bajas* (bands), and flags at the station and all men from neighbouring and distant villages including schoolboys and mukhtiars were present. They showered flowers on Mr. Gandhi and garlanded him. There was a red cloth spread at the platform for Mr. Gandhi. Surajmal Marwari of Bettiah had brought his phaeton and a horse of Puran Babu Raj, an engineer, was harnessed. It is not understood how Puran Babu lent his horse and why the railway servants allowed so much rush and show at the station.

"Mr. Gandhi was taken to Hazarimal's dharmashala accompanied by all the villagers who had come to see him. The dharmashala was nicely decorated with flags, flowers etc. Pieces of red *salus* were hung up in the air by means of rope with the following things sewed on them. The first piece of cloth had the word 'swagatam', welcome, written on it. A second piece 'Nyaya shila sarkar ki jai', *jai* to the justice-loving sarkar, was sewed. On third "Mahatma Gandhi ji ki jai' was sewed. On fourth "Shri Bharat Mata ki jai', *jai* to Mother India, was sewed and below it was written "Jin jano ne desh jiwan samarpan kardiya wai amar-pad pa gai nij bans ujwat karliya', that is, those who have sacrificed their lives for the benefit of the country, they obtained salvation and enlightened their generation.

"Rajkumar Shukla and Khendher Rai were in one carriage with Mr. Gandhi's luggage."

A mammoth meeting of villagers was expected on October 12th, because it was known that Gandhi was to announce the gist of the committee's recommendations. Mr. Lewis was perturbed because the recommendations had not yet been published and he himself was unacquainted with them. Mr. Lewis met Gandhi and said that he thought that his announcement of the committee's recommendations would be construed as Gandhi's orders to the ryots, and that a fresh crop of rumours would be started: while there would have to be a second pronouncement when the Government resolutions, possibly on different lines, were issued. Gandhi said in reply that he had the Lieutenant-Governor's permission to make the pronouncement in order to prepare the way for the Government resolutions which were to follow, and in particular to explain such unpopular clauses as compulsory *sharahbeshi* in place of the surviving *tinkathia* in a number of concerns.

Gandhi spent a couple of hours with Mr. Lewis, returned to the dharmashala, and made a public announcement of the recommendations. He left Bettiah the next day.

The planters were furious that the announcement should have been made to the ryots previous either to the publication of the report or the issue of Government order. Mr. Cox wired to the Government: "Gandhi publicly announcing committee's alleged recommendation as equivalent to Government orders thereby causing great excitement and revolt amongst ryots. We the European community of Champaran believe to be governed in supersession of all law and order by Gandhi or by the committee's unwarrantable proposals even though confirmed by Government which we confidentially anticipate that they will not be. We demand an immediate meeting between our representative and some official with full powers as requested by Champaran branch of association in order to prevent serious disturbances."

The Lieutenant-Governor declined to enter into discussion with the planters over the unanimous findings of the committee. Having considered the recommendations made in the report His Honour passed the following orders :

1. That the *tinkathia* be abolished and considered illegal.
2. That the contracts entered into between ryots and indigo concerns for growing indigo or other crops will absolutely depend on their consent.

   That the terms of such contracts shall not be more than for three years.

   That the money which will be paid under such contracts shall be according to the weight of the indigo plants. When both the parties agree the price on the weight will be determined by arbitrators.

   That money should not be paid at a rate less than that fixed by the Planters' Association from time to time and approved by the commissioner.

   That no contract will make any tenant liable for growing indigo in any particular plots of his land.
3. That the Turkaulia, Motihari and Peepra concerns have agreed that the *sharahbeshi* taken by them will be reduced up to 20 per cent in the case of Turkaulia concern and by up to 26 per cent in the case of Motihari and Peepra, from 1st Aswin 1325. In the case of the two remaining concerns also, namely, Jallah and Sirni where *sharahbeshi* has been taken, it will be reduced by 26 per cent.
4. That in those concerns where *sharahbeshi* has not been taken and the names of the ryots are entered on this condition that they are bound to grow indigo, these conditions will be abolished and in lieu thereof *sharahbeshi* will be assessed after reduction at the rate stated above and it will take effect from 1st Aswin 1325.
5. That the manager of the Bettiah Raj will not renew the leases of those villages in which *tawan* has already been taken but he can renew in case where 25 per cent of the *tawan* taken is refunded and that shall be distributed by that raj among the tenants as a part of the *tawan* refunded.
6. That in those leased villages in which *tawan* has been taken, so long as the full *tawan* realized is not refunded the Bettiah Raj should forgo for seven years any enhancement which

may have been or may be granted in the Settlement Courts in the case of those ryots from whom *tawan* has been taken.

7. That all concerned are hereby informed that *abwabs* are illegal and that it is not necessary for any tenant to pay to his *malik* or his *amla,* on their demand, anything in excess of his rent and cess finally entered in the Settlement Khatian. He is entitled to get a receipt for rent and cess without payment of any fees, *taharir* or *hisabana.*
8. That the Bihar Planters' Association will be requested to fix the minimum rate of wages of labourers required by the concerns and to send this rate to the commissioner for approval.
9. That the Bihar Planters' Association will also be requested to fix a proper rate of hire for the *sattas* relating to carts and to make a rule according to which a contract will be for not more than three to five years according to the amount advanced.

A correspondent wrote in the *Statesman* : "The local Government seem to have suddenly discovered, with the help of Mr. Gandhi, that a system extant for a hundred years is bad, and have as suddenly decided to do away with it."

The planters wielded extraordinary power and they offered stiff opposition to Government orders. Mr. Irwin declared: "That our representative signed a report of this sort is a matter which will have to be settled with him. But I hereby absolutely decline to submit to any treatment of this kind and I as publicly as possible now revoke, repudiate and withdraw the concession of 25 per cent of the *sharahbeshi* from the beginning of the coming year and will, if obliged to, spend this money in fighting this to a finish."

Mr. Kenneth Mackenzie, an ex-indigo planter from Champaran, wrote in the *Statesman*: "This action will have much more serious results than Sir Edward Gait anticipates and he, his colleagues and the members of the so-called commission, should be held collectively and individually responsible for any bloodshed that may ensue."

Sir Edward Gait, the Lieutenant-Governor, remained firm and on November 29, 1917 the Honourable Mr. Maude introduced the Champaran Agrarian Bill in the Legislative Council. In his memorable speech Mr. Maude said :

"The conditions under which indigo has been grown has been repeatedly under the notice of Government for nearly sixty years past commencing from the time when disputes in Lower Bengal led to the appointment of the Indigo Commission, as a result of which indigo rapidly disappeared in Bengal proper. In that inquiry the conditions in Tirhut were more or less a side issue. It is astonishing how even in those early times the causes of complaint were much the same. This was the state of affairs when Mr. Gandhi was induced to visit the district and the presence and actions of himself and his assistants created a tension which rendered it necessary to appoint the committee of inquiry and the recommendations of which have resulted in the bill which I am laying before the council.

"Government alone, and that only by legislation, can kill the real root of the disease, and I contend that history for fifty years and more has been building up a case for drastic action by Government and that the findings of the recent committee, findings of which I need not set forth at length because they have merely repeated once more what has been found time after time before, have merely set the keystone on the case for interference.

"Now the root of the evil is the *tinkathia* system. As the committee have put it, the *tinkathia* system has outlived its day and must perforce disappear...

"Government have no desire to strike a blow at the indigo industry, nor indeed, if they had such a desire, could they achieve it through the provisions of this bill, for the simple reason that if indigo is sound commercially it can be grown and manufactured on open business terms and yet with a good profit. If it is dependent on conditions which are unsound and oppressive the sooner it disappears from off the face of the country the better it will be."

Sir Edward Gait had a large share in getting the committee make a unanimous report and in getting the agrarian bill passed in accordance with the committee's recommendations.

The Champaran Agrarian Act received the assent of the Governor-General on May 1, 1918.

After the war the prices of indigo dropped rapidly, the industry ceased to be of any importance, and finally within a decade died out completely.

"The *tinkathia* system which had been in existence for about a century was thus abolished,'' observed Gandhi, "and with it the planters' raj came to an end. The ryots, who had all along remained crushed, now somewhat came to their own, and the superstition that the stain of indigo could never be washed out was exploded."

AFTERMATH

THROUGH Champaran a hurricane had blown and Gandhi was determined to harness the ryots' enthusiasm in bringing about constructive revolution in the villages. One of the main reasons of the sufferings of the ryots, he thought, was ignorance : even if he succeeded in securing some relief for the ryots they could not be able to get the full benefit of it and they would be caught in fresh bonds. A new consciousness was aroused but whether this was a permanent acquisition could not be said for certain. No outside agency could improve their lot unless their ignorance was dispelled. Their mode of living required a change: dirt in the villages, dirt on the roads, dirt everywhere. They had lost the capacity for organized work; they could not repair even a village road. Villagers fell an easy prey to epidemics, there being none to advise them and there being no arrangement for their treatment. When they had some leisure, they did not know how to utilize it. Men and women gossiped and children were neglected.

As Gandhi got more experience of Champaran, he became convinced that work of a permanent nature was not impossible without proper village education. "The ryots' ignorance was pathetic. They either allowed their children to roam about, or made them toil from morning to night for a couple of coppers a day. In those days a male labourer's wage did not exceed ten pice, a female's did not exceed six, a child's three. He who succeeded in earning four annas a day was considered most fortunate."

In consultation with his co-workers Gandhi decided to open primary schools in six villages. One of the conditions with the villagers was that they should provide the teachers with board and lodging while his colleagues would see to the other expenses. The village folk had hardly any cash in their hands, but they could well afford to provide foodstuffs. They expressed their readiness to contribute grain and other raw materials.

From where to get the teachers was a great problem. It was difficult to find local teachers who would work for a bare allowance or without remuneration. Gandhi's idea was not to entrust children to commonplace teachers. "Their literary qualification was not so essential as their moral fibre."

Sometime before the inquiry committee had commenced its work he had written to his friends, telling them the type of volunteers he needed for this new venture: "Their work will be the most important and lasting and, therefore, it will be the final essential stage of the mission. The volunteers have to be grown up, reliable, hard-working men who would not mind taking the spade and repairing and making roads and cleaning village cesspools and who will in their dealings with their landlords, guide the ryots aright. Six months of such training cannot fail to do incalculable good to the ryots, the workers and the country at large."

After the committee had made its report, Gandhi found time to embark on the new venture and on November 8, 1917 he returned to Champaran with Kasturba in the capacity of a volunteer. His public appeal for voluntary teachers received a ready response from Maharashtra, Gujarat and Karnatak. Mrs. Avantikabai Gokhale and Mrs. Anandibai Vaishampayan came respectively from Bombay and Poona. Babasaheb Soman and Pundalik Katgade were sent by Gangadharrao Desphande from Karnatak. Gandhi called from the Sabarmati ashram his son Devadas, Chhotalal and Surendranath. Mahadev Desai and Narhari Parikh with their wives cast in their lot with him.

Avantikabai and Anandibai were educated enough, but Durgabai Desai and Manibehn Parikh had nothing more than a bare knowledge of Gujarati, and Kasturba not even that. How were they to instruct the children in Hindi ? Gandhi explained to them that they were expected to teach the children not grammar and the three R's so much as cleanliness and good manners. He further explained that even as regards letters there was not so great difference between Gujarati, Hindi and Marathi as they imagined, and in the primary classes, at any rate, the teaching of the rudiments of the alphabet and numerals was not a difficult matter. But he did not want to stop at providing for primary education. The villages were insanitary, the lanes full of filth, the wells surrounded by mud and stink and the courtyards unbearably untidy. The older people badly needed education in cleanliness. They were all suffering from various skin diseases. So it was decided to do as much sanitary work as possible and to penetrate every department of their lives.

Doctors were needed for this work. Gandhi requested the Servants of India Society to send Dr. Deva, who readily offered his services for six months. The teachers—men and women—had all to work under Dr. Deva.

All of them had express instructions not to concern themselves with grievances against planters or with politics. People who had any complaints to make were to be referred to Gandhi. "I had seen that, even where the end might be political, but where the cause was non-political, one damaged it by giving it a political aspect and helped it by keeping it within its non-political limit. The Champaran struggle was a proof of the fact that disinterested service of the people in any sphere ultimately helps the country politically."

Gandhi told Mr. Whitty, Manager of Bettiah Raj, that his wish now was "to utilize his position and any gratitude he has earned from the ryots to introduce sanitary ideas and improve agricultural methods." He hoped that in this humanitarian work he should get the help of planters and that in their villages he should open schools. As the planters withheld their co-operation, Gandhi decided to open a school at Barharwa Lakhansen, about 20 miles to the east of Motihari, a village of Bettiah Raj, not attached to any factory. Babu Shiv Gun Mal gave his house for the school and promised monetary help also. There on November 14, 1917 Gandhi opened his first school in Champaran. The school was put in charge of Mr. Baban Gokhale, an engineer, and his wife Awantikabai Gokhale, an educationist, and Devadas, Gandhi's youngest son.

In a letter to Mr. Merriman, District Magistrate, Champaran, Gandhi wrote :

"I think that I ought to keep you informed of my doings. Having received an offer of a ready-made school in a Kham village, I opened one today in Barharwa Lakhansen near Daka. I have put there the best volunteer teachers from among those who have offered their assistance. They are Mr. and Mrs. Gokhale from Bombay. They have their independent means, and Mrs. Gokhale was doing educational work in Bombay. The nature of the work they will do I have already described to you. I am hoping with the assistance, if possible, of the heads of the respective concerns to open similar schools, one in the Peeprah *dehat* and another in Turkaulia *dehat,* and I hope to open one in the Belwa *dehat.* As this attempt is in the nature of an experiment,

I do not want to open more than four or five schools, until some definite result is obtained. I hope that I shall have the co-operation of the local officials in an experiment, which I know, is full of difficulty, but which is fraught with important consequences if it becomes successful."

He wrote again a letter to Mr. Merriman on November 19:

"In the schools I am opening, children under the age of twelve only are admitted. The idea is to get hold of as many children as possible and to give them an all-round education, that is, a knowledge of Hindi or Urdu, and through that medium, of arithmetic, rudiments of history and geography, a knowledge of simple scientific principles and some industrial training. No cut and dried syllabus has been yet prepared, because I am going along an unbeaten track. I look upon our own present system with horror and distrust. Instead of developing the moral and the mental faculties of the little children, it dwarfs them. In my experiment whilst I shall draw upon what is good in it, I shall endeavour to avoid the defects of the present system. The chief thing aimed at is contact of the children with men and women of culture and unimpeachable moral character. That to me is education. Literary training is to be used merely as a means to that end. The industrial training is designed to give the boys and girls who may come to us an additional means of livelihood. It is not intended that on completing their education, they should leave their hereditary occupation, namely, agriculture, but make use of the knowledge gained in the school to refine agriculture and the agricultural life. Our teachers will also touch the lives of the grown-up people and if at all possible penetrate the purdah. Instruction will, therefore, be given to grown-up people in hygiene, and about the advantage of joint action for the promotion of communal welfare, such as the making of village roads proper, the sinking of wells, etc. And as no school will be manned by teachers who are not men or women of good training, we propose to give free medical aid, so far as is possible. In Barharwa, for instance, Mrs. Avantikabai Gokhale who is a trained nurse and midwife and who, assisted by her husband, is in charge of the school, has already dispensed castor oil and quinine to scores of patients during the four days that she has been at work, and visited several female patients..."

On November 20 Gandhi opened another school at Bhitharwa, a village situated in the Nepal Tarai, about forty miles north-east of

Bettiah. The school consisted of a straw hut built on a land attached to a temple and donated by a sadhu who was in its charge. It was situated at a short distance from the Belwa factory managed by Mr. Amman. The school was put in charge of Mr. S. L. Soman, Mr. B. Y. Purohit, Dr. Deva and Mrs. Kasturba Gandhi.

Gandhi wrote to the district magistrate on November 22 :

"I went over to Motihari on Tuesday last and opened a school there. Mr. Soman, a public worker from Belgaum, and a B.A., LL.B., has been left in charge, and he will be assisted by Mr. Balkrishna, a young man from Gujarat. Mrs. Gandhi will join them on the 24th. Her work will be chiefly confined to moving among the women.

"I was Badhawa yesterday, and Mrs. Gokhale and my son were just returning from a visit to a dying man. They told me that the people in the district were woefully neglectful of the patients, and they believed that many preventible deaths must occur in the district for want of a simple observance of the rudimentary principles of hygiene. I know that this will not come to you as news because it is not a peculiar condition of the district in which Mrs. Gokhale is working, or of Champaran, but it is a chronic condition among the peasantry of India.

"I simply mentioned the incident in order that as soon as I have advanced a little more in my experiment, I may enlist your active sympathy and help in a department in which all can meet without reserve.

"Dr. Deva, who is a qualified and experienced surgeon and physician and Secretary of the Servants of India Society, came on Tuesday. His services have been lent for this work by the society. He has come with three more volunteers including a lady from Professor Karve's Widows' Home. Dr. Deva will chiefly supervise the medical branch of the work.

"I may state that I shall be away from Champaran for over a fortnight. Babu Brajkishore Prasad will represent me in my absence."

In his confidential report dated November 24, Mr. Merriman, the District Magistrate, wrote to Mr. Morshead, the Commissioner of Tirhut :

"The general situation gets no easier, rather the reverse. The immediate and pressing trouble centres round the question of payment of rents to factories. There is a general complaint from planters that they are unable to get in rents. I do not see any immediate prospect of the cessation of the present trouble. Meanwhile the position of the local officers is an extremely difficult one. The planter asserts that existing obligations are still binding. The ryot, relying on the vernacular notices, claims that the obligation to grow indigo, and all resultant obligations, are a dead letter, and refuses either to grow indigo, *khuski* or *lagan* or to pay any rent. He does not appreciate the subtle distinction between an executive order and a legislative enactment. To sum up, the general situation appears to be a recrudescence of excitement coinciding with Mr. Gandhi's return and the announcement of the Government resolution.

"Mr. Gandhi is again with us, though he has just written to inform me that he is going away for a fortnight. He has been very active since he arrived early in the month. He has started founding schools. I solicit instructions as to the attitude to be adopted to Mr. Gandhi and his schools and hygiene propaganda. Am I to encourage him in his work before satisfying myself of its character, or am I to adopt a neutral attitude ?

"I am not prepared as yet to make any comments either on the instruction given by him or on the character of his followers. I know nothing about them. Personally I think that if they are genuinely interested in the matter they profess, they will soon get sick of trying to teach hygiene to the Bihari cultivator. Mr. Gandhi is trying to get subscription for his schools, but has been met with a very modified enthusiasm from local Indians in this respect.

"Similarly I would like instructions as to my attitude with regard to Mr. Gandhi's other activities. He is not confining himself to hygiene and educational matters only. He has been making personal inquiries at Belwa, the place at which he has also founded a school. Mr. Gandhi has offered to make 'observations' on the case to me after it has been judicially decided. He has also been inquiring into the question of some agreements executed by the ryots of the Seerah factory. I hear from Mr. Amman that at Belwa Mr. Gandhi held a kind of inquiry and took the deposition of a complainant and some witnesses.

"As a public officer, I presume, I should welcome friendly assistance from outside. At the same time the practice of independent inquiries into cases actually pending before the courts appears to me to be open to grave charges, especially when the people concerned are, as in

Champaran, ignorant, ill-balanced and prone to untruthfulness. Mr. Gandhi himself, quite possibly, claims to be impartial, but the impartiality of many of his assistants is open to suspicion. Mr. Gandhi has, I believe, given assurance that he could only interfere in cases where he believed the ryot had been clearly victimized. But I submit Mr. Gandhi's judgement is fallible. It appears to me quite impossible to make such distinction between cases. The practice must be countenanced in all the cases or none. I ask for guidance on this point.

"With regard to the importation of volunteers from Belgaum, Gujarat and Bombay, I should like to be informed of the attitude of Government. Mr. McPherson in a letter, dated July 20, 1917, to Mr. Heycock intimated Heycock to inform Mr. Gandhi that he (Heycock) was 'not aware of the attitude Government will adopt towards the importation of volunteers'. May I now inquire if the Government will communicate to me their attitude ?"

On November 30 Gandhi wrote to the district magistrate from Motihari: "Dr. Deva tells me that in Bhitharwa and the surrounding villages nearly fifty per cent of the population is suffering from a fever which often proves fatal. Our workers are rendering all the assistance they can."

How the workers penetrated the villages and how they did the uplift work is described by Gandhi thus :

"As far as was possible we placed each school in charge of one man and one woman. These volunteers had to look after medical relief and sanitation. The womenfolk had to be approached through women.

"Medical relief was a very simple affair. Castor oil, quinine and sulphur ointment were the only drugs provided to the volunteers. If the patient showed a furred tongue or complained of constipation, castor oil was administered, in case of fever quinine was given after an opening dose of castor oil, and the sulphur ointment was applied in case of boils and itch after thoroughly washing the affected parts. No patient was permitted to take home any medicine. Wherever there was some complication Dr. Deva was consulted. Dr. Deva used to visit each centre on certain fixed days in the week.

"Quite a number of people availed themselves of this simple relief. This plan of work will not seem strange when it is remembered that the prevailing ailments were few and amenable to simple treatment, by no means requiring expert help. As for the people the arrangement answered excellently.

"Sanitation was a difficult affair. The people were not prepared to do anything themselves. Even the field labourers were not ready to do their own scavenging. But Dr. Deva was not a man easily to lose heart. He and the volunteers concentrated their energies on making a village ideally clean. They swept the roads and the courtyards, cleaned out the wells, filled up the pools near by, and lovingly persuaded the villagers to raise volunteers from amongst themselves. In some villages they shamed the people into taking up the work, and in others the people were so enthusiastic that they even prepared roads to enable my car to go from place to place. These sweet experiences were not unmixed with bitter ones of people's apathy. I remember some villagers frankly expressing their dislike for this work."

Gandhi spread his activities further by opening one more school at Madhuban on January 17, 1918. It was mainly conducted by the inmates of the Sabarmati ashram: Mr. and Mrs. Narhari Parikh, Mahadev Desai and his wife Durgabai, and Anandibai of Poona. For some time V. S. Randive and J. B. Kripalani also worked there.

These centres hummed with activity and new volunteers joined : Shankarrao Deva, B. B. Rupani, P. P. Yogi, Ramaraksha Brahmachari, Pundalik Katgade, E. V. Khsire and Shamdeva Sahai. Some paid teachers were also engaged from time to time. At Barharwa 140 boys were taught by Mr. Gokhale and about 40 girls and women by Mrs. Gokhale. Here lessons in weaving and in corporate action, such as cleaning of wells and roads, were given. At Madhuban about 100 boys and 40 girls attended the school. At Bhitharwa only about 40 children attended the school because of the distance and backwardness of the village.

Kasturba moved among the village women, taught them hygiene and sanitation and also helped her husband in surveying the conditions of the village folk. In the words of Gandhi, one of the touching incidents was as follows: "I happened to visit a small village in the vicinity of Bhitharwa and found some of the women dressed very dirtily. So I told my wife to ask them why they did not wash their clothes. She spoke to them. One of the women took her into her hut and said, 'Look now, there is no box or cupboard here containing other clothes.

The sari I am wearing is the only one I have. How am I to wash it ? Tell Mahatmaji to get me another sari, and I shall then promise to bathe and put on clean clothes every day."

The volunteers by their selfless work endeared themselves to the people. This was not to the planters' liking. One night the school at Bhitharwa was set on fire and reduced to ashes. This act of incendiarism was believed to have been done by a planter, but instead of wasting the time on inquiry, the teachers and the villagers built a brick house in place of the burnt straw hut.

All through the planters tried to get Gandhi removed from Champaran and launched a malicious propaganda through the Anglo-Indian press. Mr. Irwin, who led the campaign, wrote a letter in the *Statesman* dated January 12, 1918, criticizing even Kasturba. In reply Gandhi wrote a long letter from Motihari on January 16 :

"Mr. Irwin's latest letter published in your issue of the 12th instant compels me to court the hospitality of your columns. So long as your correspondent confined himself to matters directly affecting himself, his representations did not much matter, as the real facts were as much within the knowledge of the Government and those who are concerned with the agrarian question in Champaran, as within mine. But in the letter under notice, he has travelled outside his jurisdiction as it were, and unchivalrously attacked one of the most innocent women walking on the face of the earth (and this I say although she happens to be my wife) and has unpardonably referred to a question of the greatest moment, I mean, the cow protection question, without taking the precaution as behoves a gentleman of ascertaining facts at first hand.

"My address to the Gau-rakshini Sabha he could have easily obtained upon application to me. This at least was due to me as between man and man. Your correspondent accuses me of 'making a united attack on *saheb log* (their landlords) who salughter and eat cows daily.' This presupposes I was addressing a comparatively microscopic audience of the planters' ryots. The fact is that the audience was composed chiefly of the non-ryot class. But I had in mind a much bigger audience, and not merely the few thousand hearers before me. I spoke under a full sense of my responsibility. The question of cow protection is, in my opinion, as large as the empire to which Mr. Irwin and I belong. I know that he is a proud father of a young lad of twenty-four, who has received by his gallantry the unique honour of colonelcy at his age. Mr. Irwin can, if he will, obtain a greater honour for himself by studying the cow question and taking his full share in its solution. He will, I promise, be then much better occupied, than when he is dashing off his misrepresentations to be published in the press and most unnecessarily preparing to bring 2,200 cases against his tenants for the sake of deriving the questionable pleasue of deeming me responsible for those cases.

"I said at the meeting that the Hindus had no warrant for resenting the slaughter of cows by their Mahomedan brethren who kill them from religious conviction, so long as they themselves were a party to the killing by inches of thousands of cattle who were horribly ill-treated by their Hindu owners, to the drinking of milk drawn from cows in the inhuman dairies of Calcutta and so long as they calmly contemplated the salughter of thousands of cattle in the slaughter-houses of India for providing beef for the European and Christian residents of India. I suggested that the first step towards procuring full protection for cows was to put their own house in order by securing absolute immunity from ill-treatment of their cattle by Hindus themselves, and then to appeal to the Europeans to abstain from beef-eating whilst resident in India, or at least to procure beef from outside India. I added that in no case could the cow protection propaganda, if it was to be based upon religious conviction, tolerate a sacrifice of Mahomedans for the sake of saving cows, that the religious method of securing protection from Christians and Mahomedans alike was for Hindus to offer themselves a willing sacrifice of sufficient magnitude to draw out the merciful nature of Christians and Mahomedans. Rightly or wrongly worship of the cow is ingrained in the Hindu nature and I see no escape from a most bigoted and sanguinary strife over this question between Christians and Mahomedans on the one hand and Hindus on the other except in the fullest recognition and practice by the Hindus of the religion of ahimsa, which it is my self-imposed and humble mission in life to preach. Let the truth be faced. It must not be supposed that Hindus feel nothing about the cow slaughter going on for the European. I know that their wrath is today being buried under the awe inspired by the English rule. But there is not a Hindu throughout the length and breadth of India who does not expect one day to free his land from cow slaughter. But contrary to the genius of Hinduism as I know it he would not mind forcing even at the point of the sword either the

Christian or the Mahomedan to abandon cow slaughter. I wish to play my humble part in preventing such a catastrophe and I thank Mr. Irwin for having provided me with an opportunity of inviting him and your readers to help me in my onerous mission. The mission may fail to prevent cow slaughter. But there is no reason why by patient plodding and consistent practice it should not succeed in showing the folly, the stupidity and the inhumanity of committing the crime of killing a fellow human being for the sake of saving a fellow animal.

"So much on behalf of the innocent cow. A word only for my innocent wife who will never even know the wrong your correspondent has done her. If Mr. Irwin would enjoy the honour of being introduced to her he will soon find out that Mrs. Gandhi is a simple woman, almost unlettered, who knows nothing of the two bazars mentioned by him, even as I knew nothing of them until very recently and some time after the establishement of the rival bazar, referred to by Mr. Irwin. He will then further assure himself that Mrs. Gandhi has had no hand in its establishment and is totally incapable of managing such a bazar. Lastly he will at once learn that Mrs. Gandhi's time is occupied in cooking for and serving the teachers conducting the school established in the *dehat* in question, in distributing medical relief and in moving amongst the women of the *dehat* with a view to giving them an idea of simple hygiene. Mrs. Gandhi, I may add, has not learnt the art of making speeches or addressing letters to the press.

"As to the rest of the letter, the less said the better. It is so full of palpable misrepresentations that it is difficult to deal with them with sufficient self-restraint. I can only say that I am trying to the best of my ability to fulfil the obligation, I hold myself under, of promoting goodwill between planters and ryots, and if I fail it would not be due to want of efforts on my part, but it would be largely, if not entirely, due to the mischievous propaganda Mr. Irwin is carrying on openly and some others *sub rosa* in Champaran in order to nullify the effect of the report published by the Agrarian Committee, which was brought into being not as Mr. Irwin falsely suggests at my request, but by the agitation carried on, as your files would demonstrate, by Mr. Irwin and his friends of the Anglo-Indian Association. If he is wise he will abide by his written word, voluntarily and after full discussion and deliberation, given by him at Ranchi."

The Anglo-Indian press, especially the *Pioneer* and the *Statesman* mainly gave the news of the war and they were scared by the reverses of the allies and the revolution in Russia. The only news they gave about India was regarding the happenings in Champaran. It was rather curious that they sided with Gandhi during the South African struggle and wrote editorials in sympathy with the indentured labour, but in the case of Champaran they put all their weight on the side of the planters and carried on a virulent propaganda against Gandhi. The nationalist press had not realized the importance of the South African struggle, but now they sided with the ryots in Champaran and gave its fullest support to Gandhi. Paying tribute to Gandhi, the nationalist press quoted the apt article by Professor Gilbert Murray published in the *Hibbert Journal* of January 1918 :

"Let me take present-day instance of this battle between a soul and. a Government, a very curious instance, because it is almost impossible without more knowledge than most people in England possess to say who was wrong and who right.

"Persons in power should be very careful how they deal with a man who cares nothing for sensual pleasure, nothing for riches, nothing for comfort or praise or promotion, but is simply determined to do what he believes to be right. He is a dangerous and uncomfortable enemy because his body, which you can always conquer, gives you so little purchase upon his soul".

By his selflessness and indomitable courage Gandhi put new life into the ryots of Champaran. In February 1918 he had to rush to Ahmedabad to lead the textile labourers on strike there and the distressed peasants in Kheda. His hope of putting constructive work on a permanent footing was not fulfilled. "The volunteers had come for temporary periods, I could not secure any more from outside, and permanent honorary workers from Bihar were not available. As soon as my work in Champaran finished, work outside, which had been preparing in the meantime, drew me away. The few months' work in Champaran, however, took such deep root that its influence in one form or another is to be observed even today", wrote Gandhi in his autobiography.

Gandhi attached such a great importance to the Champaran struggle that he once said: Those who would know my method of organizing kisans may profitably study the movement in Champaran when stayagraha was tried for the first time in India with the result all India knows. It became a mass movement which remained wholly non-violent from start to finish. It affected over twenty lakhs of kisans. The struggle centred round one specific grievance which was a century old. There had been several violent revolts to get rid of the grievance. They were suppressed. The non-violent remedy succeeded in full in six months. The kisans of Champaran became politically conscious without any direct effort. The tangible proof they had of the working of non-violence to remove their grievance drew them to the Congress and they gave a good account of themselves during the civil disobedience campaigns."

In Champaran, where the sages in ancient days did penance, Gandhi realized the mission of his life and forged a weapon by which India could be made free.